FREEDOM FROM HUNGER

Freedom from Hunger

(Concept & Case Study)

S.N. MISRA
SHIBALAL MEHER

ANMOL PUBLICATIONS PVT. LTD.
NEW DELHI - 110 002 (INDIA)

ANMOL PUBLICATIONS PVT. LTD.
4374/4B, Ansari Road, Daryaganj
New Delhi - 110 002
Ph.: 23261597, 23278000
Visit us at: www.anmolpublications.com

Freedom from Hunger

First Published, 2004

ISBN 81-261-2019-3

PRINTED IN INDIA

Published by J.L. Kumar for Anmol Publications Pvt. Ltd., New Delhi - 110 002 and Printed at Mehra Offset Press, Delhi.

Contents

Foreword

The report makes a detailed analysis regarding the constraints that hinder development in spite of huge investments made in anti-poverty programmes. It also gives some concrete suggestions for all-round rural development with improvement in agriculture, irrigation, non-farm occupations, infrastructure and so on. I need not again repeat the points mentioned in the study. I want to make a few comments of general nature which are relevant to the present discussion.

Though most of the Anti-Poverty Programmes are basically employment oriented or security based, they are basically ad hoc and not well designed or planned. We cannot eliminate such anti-poverty programmes in view of the fact that some short-term measures are necessary to provide some assistance to the poor or destitute. But most of the funds allocated for such programmes become infructous thanks to the total bureaucratic control over it. If the same amount can be put with the village community where every one is associated with the given activity, and not monopolised by the Village Pradhan as happens in case of Jawahar Rozagar Yojana, the picture would be different.

Further, the target approach treats poverty as an individual tragedy. But the colossal poverty that exists in rural areas is a problem with a clear socio-economic roots and causes. The target approach is just like identifying some families who are affected by some epidemics like cholera or malaria and taking measures to eradicate such epidemics. This is just attacking the symptom instead of taking measures which can prevent such maladies. Anti-poverty programmes, therefore, help to postpone the inevitable spread of the disease.

This implies that poverty and hunger cannot be eliminated without sustained productive investment in rural development. Doles cannot remove poverty and hunger. Apart from the fact that the amount of doles required for the purpose is quite large, doles or subsidies become the real rallying point of various agents like officers, bankers, local politicians who compete with each other to grab a major portion of the amount. Since anti-poverty programmes in the short period cannot be dispensed with, they should be integrated with different types of developmental work so that after a particular period their necessity will be less important.

Take the case of IRDP which is the Kingpin of APPs. This is neither integrated sectorally or otherwise nor related to rural development pertaining to agriculture, irrigation, non-farm occupations, forestry, fishery and so on. Additional investment in these sectors will provide the necessary impetus for growth. Therefore, separate funds have to be provided for these developmental works. But if somehow anti-poverty programmes can be integrated with such developmental works, it will be easier to find funds for development and reduce the necessity of subsidies.

Again, there is a great necessity to improve the operational efficiency of both APPs and permanent developmental works. World Bank Report (1997, p. 33) indicates that the cost of providing one rupee of APP services to the poor ranges from Rs. 2/- to Rs. 7/-. How can you provide adequate benefit to the poor with such heavy administrative cost along with booties to various intermediaries who are involved in the process? The responsibilities of both APP work and permanent development work are quite heavy, demanding and sometimes baffling. We cannot entirely depend on governmental agencies for such a stupendous work. Governmental agencies are quite good for regulation, not for development. As such there is need to evolve some local developmental agencies which can bear the brunt of all round development and meet the temporary needs of the poor people who deserve some assistance. This needs the adoption of a participatory approach covering with the selection of different development programmes and projects, including consideration of anti-poverty programmes and their implementation. If this role is operated through a new rural development structure starting from Village Development Committees (VDCs), operational mechanism of both long-term developmental programmes and short-term measures for assistance can be improved considerably.

In the end, I want to thank Dr. S.N.Misra, the Project Director and his associates Dr. Sibalal Meher along with their research associates and investigators who have taken immense trouble in preparing this report. The B.D.O. and his co-workers also deserve our thanks for their ungrudging help and assistance in collection of necessary data from the block. The people in the area have been helpful in explaining to us the working of the different APPs and developmental works. I personally visited some of the village and I have seen the abysmal poverty in which they live. Yet they have spared some time to meet us and tell us their worries and constraints. We are really thankful to them for their cooperation. And the most important agency which deserves our sincere thanks is the Panchayati Raj Department which has given us the study without imposing any pre-conditions. I hope our report will provide some policy implications which will guide the development for improving the future design of APPs and developmental works.

—Baidyanath Misra
Chairman & Hon. Director
NKC Centre for Dev. Studies

Preface

Poverty and Hunger are the two basic human problems that need immediate solution. Hunger is the cause of poverty. Hunger can be either transitory or chronic and it is the latter which demands definite and concrete policy measures for overcoming the same. Hunger is caused by people having neither the capacity to produce food nor the income to pay for it. In developing countries like India hunger is not due to non-availability of food but the inaccessibility of people to buy food. Besides, people have no access to socio-economic entitlements like nutrition, education, health and sanitation etc. This is also true in case of Orissa, where more poor and hungry people reside.

In order to overcome Poverty and Hunger at the sub national level pertaining to a state, the Government of Orissa has launched a project titled **'Freedom from Hunger'** with the following aims: conceptualisation and identification of people who are hungry, measures adopted by the State Government for removing poverty and hunger under Five Year Plans, identification of critical gaps and missing links in the governmental measures targeted for removing hunger and poverty, locating Catalysts of growth or growth inducing agents and measures to improv them, allocation of funds in growth inducing sectors and prioritisation of such investment in each sector etc.

In Orissa the study was conducted in two underdeveloped blocks like Begunia block of newly formed Khurda district and Laikera block of Jharsuguda district. While Begunia is a non-tribal block, Laikera is a tribal block. The responsibility of undertaking the study in Begunia block was shouldered by us. The period of study was from November 1996 to May 1997.

During the course of the study we have received ungrudging

support, cooperation and guidance from several quarters and we feel it appropriate to record our appreciation to all of them.

First of all we express our deep sense of gratitude to Professor Baidyanath Misra, Chairman and Director of the Institute for taking keen and active interest from the formulation of project proposal to its final completion. As every stage, his valuable suggestion, guidance and motivation were available to us liberally, without which the work would not been completed within the scheduled time. More particularly we are grateful to him for scrutinising and reviewing the entire work in spite of his onerous responsibility and busy schedules of work in the Centre.

We take this opportunity to express our sincere thanks to Sri S. Bandhopadhaya, former Principal Secretary for taking active interest in sponsoring such a type of study, having national and global importance to be undertaken by our Centre. We also express our thanks to the present Principal Secretary and other officials of Panchayati Raj department for giving us constant support and guidance for undertaking the study.

Our thanks are also due to the Block Development Officer Sri Guru Charan Prasad, Welfare Extension Officer, Progress Assistant, and Agricultural Extension Officer, Begunia Block for providing us with all the relevant information and data about the block besides rendering unstinted cooperation for the successful launching of the Project.

We also like to thank the Secretaries and Sarapanchas of all the twenty Panchayats of Begunia Block for providing with us all the necessary information, data and material about their respective Panchayats. Even some of them travelled with us to remote rural areas of the Panchayats.

The Research Investigators; Sri Sanatan Swain, Sri S.K.Sahu, Sri Chandrakanta Mishra, Miss Madhuri Padhy and Sri Debadutta Sahu deserve our special thanks for undertaking the field study even under inconvenient situations. It is because of their sincere effort, dedication and commitment that the field study and the processing of field level data were completed in the scheduled time.

Last but not the least our thanks are due to all the office staff of the NKC Centre for Development Studies who cooperated with us at every stage of our work. Particularly the services rendered by Sri Srikanta Rath, Assistant Administrative Officer, Sri Debabrata Sahoo, Senior Steno to Director, Sri N.K.Mishra, Junior Stenographer and Mrs. Kasturi Mishra, Typist need special mention.

—S.N. Misra & S. Meher

1

Poverty, Hunger and Economic Development: A Theoretical Discourse

In the Twenty-first Century, the world still faces a crucial challenge to meet the most basic human right, 'Freedom from Hunger'. How can it be ensured that hunger will cease to exist among all the individuals?

Despite the existence of sufficient food supplies in the world, at least 700 million people do not have access to sufficient food for a healthy and productive life[1]. In India, about 21 per cent of its people are starving even though its food supply is sufficient to cover their minimum needs[2]. The world now produces more food per capita than it did a decade ago. Of course, even if current supplies can, in theory, match current minimum needs, the adequacy of future supplies is not assured. Seeking to match the food supply with the demands for a fast-growing world population is a huge cost. However, the problem is that hunger is not just about the food supply. Trying to guarantee a minimum diet for today's hungry even when the food is available is just as great a challenge[3].

What is Hunger?

Hunger is the worst form of deprivation of a human being. It is defined as an individual's inability to eat sufficient food in terms of calories and nutrients to lead a healthy and active life[4]. It exists because poor people cannot gain access to available food. This occurs at global, national, regional and household levels: Food may be available at the global level, but individual countries can go short; sufficient food may be available on the market at national or regional levels, but some households go hungry because they cannot purchase it; Sufficient food may be available at a household level, but some individuals go hungry because they do not have access to it[5]. Hunger is, therefore, as much about access as it is about supply. Undernutrition and starvation can occur in the midst of plenty.

According to Amartya Sen, hunger is not due to the lack of supply of food but more due to the inability of the people to buy food. Hunger can coexist with a plentiful supply of food in the economy and the markets. It can be best seen in terms of failure of people's entitlements, that is, their failure to establish command over an adequate amount of food and other necessities. [6]

Hunger is directly related to both availability and accessibility of food items to individuals and family members. The accessibility of the food items is a function of availability of money. The availability of money in turn is a function of remuneration. The remuneration is a function of nature of job, employment, duration of employment, etc. The nature of employment is a function of education on the one hand, and training received, experience and the capability to compete with others on the other hand. There are various other factors that determine the nature of casual relationship, one bears with money accrual system. The quality and nature of the education one receives from the childhood depends upon the relative position of parents. Thus, net effect is poverty, which is consequence of numerous vicious circles interacting on the individuals in the poverty as well as on the group and posterity of poor.[7]

Hunger is perhaps the most obvious manifestation of food insecurity resulting from a complex combination of these factors, compounded by institutional and policy failure. In other words, it is a combination of the degree of poverty, the degree of risk of failing to secure local food and income, and the chance of receiving external assistance that defines food insecurity.[9]

A clear distinction must be made between hunger and poverty. Hunger is a recurring feature of absolute poverty that has long-term (chronic), short-term (acute), and seasonal (transitory) dimensions[10]. On the other hand, the more common definition of poverty is in terms of inadequacy of income (e.g., a person's income level falling below the poverty line)[11]. Hence, hunger is a special case of poverty.

It is, therefore, useful to separate out and address the issue of hunger as a major element of broader problems of poverty and food insecurity.

Sen has juxtaposed famine and endemic deprivation as the two essential dimensions of hunger.[12] Famine is acute and dramatic, but involves a relatively small proposition of hungry. On the other hand, endemic deprivation is largely but accounts for most of the world's hungry. Between these two, endemic deprivation is the most important dimension of hunger. Besides the above two forms of hunger, it also takes other forms of malnutrition. Hence, there are three basic manifestations of hunger and malnutrition.

1. Starvation: a life-threatening condition caused by insufficient food that is generally associated with acute situations like famine.

2. Chronic hunger or undernutrition: a persistent lack of calories (enough food) that may impair the ability to lead a fully healthy and active life.

3. Other forms of malnutrition: a pathological condition resulting from inadequacy of calories, protein and micronutrients, often in combination with diseases, parasites, and inadequate knowledge about nutrition.[13]

The chronically hungry or undernourished can be divided into three groups: Small and marginal farmer, and rural landless workers; unemployed; and chronically ill, the aged, the crippled and the orphaned[14]. While the first group can take part in the development process, the unemployed in the second group remains at the fringe of economic development. Poverty marked by chronic under nutrition, poor health, insanitary drinking water, large families, and crowd housing increases their vulnerability to infectious diseases, stifles their motivation, and reduces their capacity to work and study. For them development at the aggregate level offers little relief. An increase in total food production may not improve their nutritional status by much, because they would still not have enough money to buy food. People in the third group will have to rely on direct help, including such basic assistance as free food, housing and health care.

Causes of Hunger

There are a number of causes of hunger. Yunus points out that although inability to access food is the immediate cause of hunger the real cause in most incidents of hunger is lack of ability to pay for food. He mentions that hunger is a symptom of poverty. If we can root out poverty, we root out the systematic cause of hunger.[15]

IFPRI's companion paper portrays the long-term relationship between root causes and symptoms of hunger. The paper indicates that povery, including natural and man-made shocks, is a root cause of hunger[16]. It also depicts the broad interactions between policy failures, resource poverty, disasters and the population transition that impact on hunger. Within this context, the main reasons why people are hungry are lack of assets and resources to produce enough food, lack of income to buy enough food, and lack of specific essential nutrients and knowledge. These conditions are in turn affected by the natural resource environment and the economic and resource environment in which the hungry live. These influence the level and nature of employment; and the availability of social services, especially health, housing, water supply, and education.

Issues of Hunger

The concern with global hunger is most often stimulated by short-term phenomena such a famines, which activate people's humanitarian concerns, or by disruptions in the world food supply, which spark Malthusian anxieties of a world running short of food. While these are important elements of hunger problem, they are in sense transitory. When the anxiety diminishes people tend to feel that the problem has been solved. However, the major cause of hunger is what Sen calls endemic deprivation, for which the solutions have less to do with global food production and more to do with poverty and inequality and employment growth, and distribution within countries and in the world as a whole.[17]

A number of concerns have become prominent on the agenda as overcoming hunger. Some of these are equity, sustainability, participation and the role of women.[18]

1. Equity: Concern of Equity the WDR of 1992 recognises that the burden of poverty is spread unevenly—among the regions of the developing world, among countries within those regions, and among localities within those countries. Two issues are involved for this. Harry Walters presents the following issues that are put forth recently for overcoming hunger.

* One is recognition that greater equity in the distribution of assets needed to produce food or income would result in less hunger. This view focuses on the redistribution of existing resources as a means to overcome hunger.

* The other issue emphasises that raising hungry people's command over food through more productive employment and incomes will raise people out of poverty and reduce hunger, which focuses on the future.

Each approach has strong proponents. Overcoming hunger now and in the future requires greater attention to equity in people's access to food and the resources to produce it, and the measures to enable them to escape from poverty.

2. Sustainability: Sustainability has become an increasingly pressing concern for viable approaches to development, and is particularly important for overcoming hunger. The prevalence of hunger among poor farmers and their families, often in environmentally fragile regions, makes clear the link between unsustainable natural resource exploitation and meeting household food needs. The 1992 World Development Report (WDR) highlighted this link: "alleviation of poverty is both a moral imperative and a prerequisite for environmental sustainability. The poor are both victims and agents of environmental damage" (WDR, 1992). Thus, environmental degradation is an important hunger (and poverty) issue.

3. Participation: As anti-hunger efforts increasingly focus on people who are excluded and marginalized, the issue of participation and empowerment becomes increasingly crucial to their success. Overcoming hunger will not be achieved solely by donors, governments, or concerned outsiders. The poor who are hungry must be key players, not only as recipients of assistance, but also as producers. Ensuring that the poor participate in the design of programmes and projects to alleviate their own hunger is far from common practice.

4. Role of Women: Securing the full participation of women is also essential to overcome hunger. Women and children suffer the most from hunger. Women are not only central to the preparation and distribution of food within household, but in many parts of the world they are the major producers of food. Often the key entry point in targeted food and nutrition interventions is through women to their children. Finding ways to enhance women's participation in food production equally important.

While considering the hunger issues two larger perspectives of hunger, viz. political nature of hunger problem, and the practical possibilities for action, should be considered. People often see the hunger problem in its direct food production or nutrition dimensions, but it has also important political dimensions. People are hungry because they are poor, and because they are poor their participation in the political process is weak. At some point all solutions for overcoming hunger, no matter how seemingly technical, must face the reality that transfers of income or resources, either to consume or produce food or to gain access to other sources of income and social services, are needed. Access to these economic and social opportunities are ultimately issues of the functioning political systems. Proposals for overcoming hunger often call for political will, but how to achieve this is left vague.[19]

Previous Hunger Initiatives

Hunger has been the focus of international policy pronouncements and conferences for a long time. Development institutions such as the World Bank, the International Fund for Agricultural Development (IFAD), the World Food Programme (WFP), the Food and Agricultural Organisation of the United Nations (FAO) and the United Nations Children's Fund (UNICEF), along with governments and non-governmental organisations (NGOs), have emphasised the hunger focus of their assistance programmes.[20]

Overcoming hunger was a central issue at the time of the establishment of the FAO in 1945. In the 1960s, a number of major conferences were held in the United States to overcome food shortages and hunger in South Asia, China and the former USSR. Among these, the strategy for the Conquest of Hunger by the Rockefeller Foundation (1963), the World Food Problem by the U.S. President's Science Advisory Committee (1967), and Overcoming World Hunger by the American Assemble (1969), more significant. The discussion of these conferences resulted in detailed studies of the causes of hunger and related food problems. These contributed to serve the green revolution, which produced dramatic increase in food production and reductions in hunger in South and Southeast Asia and in Latin America in the 1960s and 1970s.[21]

The World Food Conference held in Rome in 1974 is widely claimed to have been a major milestone in drawing attention to the hunger problem in developing countries. It gave rise to the most comprehensive effort ever to address the global and hunger problem. It also established three international organisations to deal with the hunger problem: The World Food Council, the FAO committee on World Food Security, and the Consultative Group on Investment in Food Production. All these organisations were either meant to address food supply issues or ended up doing so for a good part of their existence. The relationship between hunger and poverty was, however, only tangentially addressed.[22]

The 1989 Bellagio, Italy, Conference proposed a sharply focused objective to reduce hunger by one-half in the 1990s[23]. Similarly, conferences including the UNICEF Children's Summit (1990), the Rio Conference on Environment and Development (1992), and the International Conference on Nutrition (1992) addressed hunger and endorsed recommendations and targets for its elimination or reduction.[24]

Despite the above initiatives, the goal of overcoming or eradicating hunger remains elusive. This is due to the following missing links.[25]

* There is little support for each global mechanism to reduce hunger as either a world food board or a world food council.

* Hunger problems are country specific. Within counties they have also regional, community, and household specific ele ments.

* Many problems have to be resolved at multiple levels.

* Overcoming hunger is clearly not a one-dimensional problem It is not simply an issue of food and its allocation.

* Despite the improved knowledge about who is hungry and how hunger can be reduced, many differences persist prac-titioners and policymakers.

* Global action on hunger requires multiple decisions at many levels. Unless governments put in place mechanisms to iden tify the hungry and initiate actions to reduce hunger, little can be accomplished. At the same time, unless the interna tional community is prepared to support national efforts and to address those hunger issues that are influences by interna tional action, national efforts will be constrained. Currently, mechanisms focused on over coming hunger are weak at both levels.

Approaches to Reduce Poverty and Hunger

There are three broad, overlapping approaches to reduce hunger. These are (a) economic growth (b) Poverty reduction and (c) pub-lic provisioning. Dreze and Sen grouped these approaches into two categories, viz., growth-mediated security and support-led security[26].

The first strategy, i.e., growth-mediated security, takes the form of fast growth of per capita national real income and the use of the gains of this growth to enhance the living conditions of the people on a wide basis. Clearly growth by itself is not enough, but it is nevertheless essential. Growth reduces hunger to the extent that it reduces income poverty (i.e. the poor are active participants in the growth process, and is used to finance public support is key areas where markets work poorly, notably, in the provision of basic health, nutrition, and education services. Such an approach is more directly linked to concerns with empowerment and equity than might appear on the suface[27]. This is practised in the countries like Korea, Hong

Kong, etc. in Asia.

The other strategy, i.e. support-led security, taken the form of promoting through direct public support— entitlements to education, health care and food without waiting for the per capita national income to rise to a high level through economic growth. There are evidences in countries such as Sri Lanka or in parts of countries such as Kerala, India, where incomes are low and growth has been slow, but there is high degree of equity or targeted social programmes focusing on food, health, and education.[28]

The above two strategies have the common feature of marshalling public action, particularly in extensive use of public provisioning (especially in health care, basic education and food distribution), to enhance living conditions.[29]

Public action can help to eradicate the dreadful, and tenacious problems of starvation and hunger in the world in which one live, but that for this to happen, we must see public action in a broad perspective — involving not just the government, but also the public it self— in all its manifold economic, social, and political activities.[30]

Basu has discussed whether 'direct action' for mitigating the poverty, problem could be fruitful or would it be necessary to wait for the benefits of growth to 'trickle down.' He has argued that direct action is possible and desirable. To pursue this objective it is not necessary to sacrifice growth. Different Policy instruments are available for achieving higher growth and greater equity. The direct action programmes, according to Basu, take the form of economic action, but their success depends greatly on their political background — in particular the ability to remove the political constraints that often make them ineffective or degenerate.[31]

Therefore, growth is not sufficient for eliminating poverty and hunger. A combination of growth-mediated and support-led security is needed to avoid the contradiction.in entitlement suffered by vulnerably groups and to eradicate poverty land chronic hunger.

As has been discussed earlier that poverty is a root cause of hunger, to eliminate hunger it is necessary to eradicate poverty. There are various ways by which poverty can be eradicated. These are: (i) trickle down effect of general economic growth, (ii) creation of income earning opportunities for poor and vulnerable groups, (iii) Streamlining of PDS, (iv) direct income transfer in the form of old age pension and unemployment allowances, etc., and (v) increasing the power of entitlement and capacity of the weaker sections of the society. These types of measures have been implemented in various states in India, but the outcome of the programmes is different is different across the states.

In the state of Orissa various measures and programmes to eradicate poverty have been implemented during different plan periods viz., (i) In agriculture through consolidation of holdings, supply of inputs, marketing of agricultural products and extension of irrigation, etc., (ii) in allied sector such as plantation, diary, poulty piggery and horticulture through the creation of vital infrastructure in the form of chilling plants, collection and marketing of milk products, supply of feeds and fodders etc., (iii) in rural non-farm sector through the implementation of DPAP programmes etc., (iv) in population control through planning programme and special benefit to green card holder, (v) in targeted programmes for poor through IRDP, TRYSEM, DWCRA, JRY, EAS, MWS, IAY and others, (iv) in health sector through mobile health service, ICDS, etc., (vi) in education through mid-dasy meal scheme, residential school in every ITDA block, TLC, DPEP and others, and (viii) in infrastructure through provision of road communication to every village, water and electricity provision to SC/ST households at subsidised rates and various other measures. No doubt these measures have an impact in reducing the intensity of poverty in the state but the rate of reduction is in fact slower compared to other states like Andhra Pradesh, Gujarat, West Bengal and Kerala.

Thus, many programmes were launched in the state to eradicate poverty but unfortunately these programmes have not been sustained for long. It is a pity that even after 50 years of planning about 47.15 per cent of people in Orissa are still living below the poverty line[32]. It is the highest state in India in respect of the poverty ratio. Some blocks in Orissa typify in many respects the limited success of various uncoordinated and mere targets reaching policy measures pursued to eradicate poverty. People in these blocks have suffered mainly due to constant neglect, multiple deprivation and exploitation through outside traders, local feudal elements, power brokers and the state bureaucracy. There are also leakage in the implementation of the targeted programmes for the poor. Instead of benefiting the real poor for whom the programmes are meant, the targeted programmes have mainly benefited the well-to-do amongst the poor and rich at the grass root level. Along with 'chronic' poverty there is prevalence of 'transitory' poverty in some underdeveloped blocks which leads to hunger, starvation and in some cases distress migration. In this context the situation of Begunia Block, in the district of Khurda, is alarming. About 83 per cent of families were lying below the poverty line during 1992 as per the survey conducted by the Block. Both chronic poverty and transitory poverty are found to be deep seated in the Block.

In view of the seriousness of the problem which is observed both at the state level in general and Begunia Block in particular, it is considered more appropriate and timely to chalk out a plan of action that would be more effective and suitable for eradicating hunger from the block within a stipulated period.

Plan of the Study

The present study has been organised in the following way. Chapter one is the Introductory Chapter and is in the form of a prologue. It outline the essential features of the study. In the second Chapter an attempt is made to give an overview of the socio-economic features of Begunia Block selected for the study. In the third Chapter we present an account of the different aspects of the methodology adopted for this study. Fourth Chapter has analysed various aspects of government programmes and measures, which are now being implemented in the Block. We have tried to find out different missing links and critical gaps in the programmes studied. In the fifth Chapter, an attempt has been made to compare the socio-economic life style of the sample beneficiaries and non-beneficiaries. In the sixth Chapter, catalysts for growth have been identified and measures to promote them are suggested. Allocation of resources in these growth inducing sectors and the prioritisation of their investment in each sector are also discussed here. The last chapter being the concluding part of the study and in the nature of an epılogue, some policy prescriptions have been suggested for a hunger free block.

NOTES

1. Patrik Webb and Joachim Von Braun, 'Ending Hunger Soon: Concepts and Priorities, in ismail Serageldin and Pierre Landle-ll-Mills (eds), *Overcoming Global Hunger,* The World Bank, Washington, D.C.1994.
2. Sujata Madhok, 'World Food Summit: Half a Loaf for the Hunger', *Kurukshètra,* Dec.1996 p. 7.
3. Webb and Bram, *op. cit.*
4. *Ibid.*
5. *Ibid,* p. 203.
6. Amartya Sen, *Poverty and Famines,* U.K.Clarendon Press, Oxford, 1981; The Political Economy of Hunger.'in Seragelding and Landell-Mills (eds). *Overcoming Global Hunger*. The World Bank, Washington, D.C 1994, p. 86; Jean Dreze and Amartya Sen, *Hunger and Public Action,* Clarendon Press, Oxford,1989.
7. R.Gedam, *Poverty in India,* Deep and Deep Publication, New Delhi, 1995, p. 413.
8. *Ibid.*
9. Harry Walters, 'Overcoming Global Hunger: An Issues Paper, in Serageldin and Landell-Mills (eds). *Overcoming Global Hunger,* The World Bank, Washington, D.C., 1994, p. 128.10. Webb and Braum, *op. cit.*
11. Dreze and Sen, *op. cit* p. 9.
12. Amartya Sen, *Public Action to Remdy Hunger*, The Hungeer Project, London 1990.
13. Harry Walters, *op. cit.*
14. *Ibid.*
15. Muhammad Yunus, 'Lessons of Experience, in Serageldin and Landell-Mills (eds). *Overcoming Global Hunger,* The World Bank, Washington D.C.1994 p. 4.
16. Harry Walters, *op. cit.*
17. *Ibid.* p. 130.
18. *Ibid,* pp. 130-31.
19. *Ibid,* p.13
20. S. Rentlinger and Amd Castillo, 'Addressing: A Historical Perspect--ive of International Initiatives', in Seragelding and Landell-Mills (eds). *Overcoming Global Hunger,* The World Bank, Washington, D.C 194, p. 147.
21. Harry Walters, *op. cit,* P.132.
22. Rentlinger and Castillo. *op cit,* pp. 152-53.
23. *The Bellagio Declaration: Overcoming Hunger in the1990s,* Bellagio,

Italy, Nov. 1989.

24. Rentlinger and Castillow, *op.cit. p.* 134,
25. Harry Walters, *op. cit. p.* 134
26. Dreze and Sen, *op. cit.*
27. Harry Walters, *op. cit.*, p. 135.
28. Dreze and Sen, *op. cit.*
29. *Ibid.*
30. Amartya Sen, 1994, *op. cit.*
31. Kaushik Basu, 'The Elimination of Endemic Poverty in South Asia: Some Policy Options', in Jean Dreze, Amartya Sen and Athar Hussain (eds). *The Political Economy of Hunger,* Clarendon Press, Oxford, 1995.
32. Planning Commission Estimate (1999-2000), Government of India.

2

Overview of the Study Area

Begunia, located in the eastern part of Orissa is an underdeveloped Block in the district of Khurda and lies in the latitude of 20^0 North and longitude of 86^0 East. It is stituated on the State Highway-1 running between Khurda and Nayagarh. It is 20 km. away from Khurda and 45 km. away from the State Capital, Bhubaneswar. It is bounded on the north by Cuttack district, on the south by Tangi Block, on the east by Khurda Block, and on the west by Bolagada Block and Nayagarh District. The block spreads over an area of 39.7 sq.km., which accounts for about 10.6 per cent of the total area in the district.

The Block has 20 Gram Panchayats with 172 Revenue Villages. It has three parts: Central, North and South. The Central region has 4 Gram Panchayats, while the North and South regions have 5 and 11 Gram Panchayats respectively. Most of the main offices, including the block, are located in the central region. The list of Panchayats and Revenue Villages selected under different Panchayats and by different regions are given in Annexure-I

Demographic Scenario

Begunia block has a total population of 1.03 lakh (According to 1991 Census) which constitutes 6.87 per cent of the total population in the district and 0.33 per cent of the total population in the State. The economy is mainly an agrarian one and all the people live in the rural areas. The S.C. and S.T. population in the block is around 21.0 per cent which is higher than the district (18.76 per cent) average, though significantly lower than the state (38.41 per cent). However, the S.T. population (11.45 per cent) in the block is higher than the S.C. population (9.54 per cent) in contrast to that in the district and the State.

The density of population in the block is 295 per sq.km., which is higher than the State (203). The annual compound growth rate of population from 1971 to 1991 in the block is 1.79 per cent, while it is 1.85 per cent in the State. The growth rate of S.C. & S.T. population in the Block is 2.45 per cent, which is higher than the overall growth rate of population during the same period.

The sex ratio in the block is 983 females per 1000 males according to 1991 Census. This is significantly higher than the district (903) as well as the State (971). However, the sex ratio in the block has declined overtime from 1026 in 1971 to 983 in 1991.

Land, Water and other Natural Resources

A major constraint on growth in Begunia seems to be the poor endowments of natural resources, which are unevenly distributed and inefficiently managed. The rainfall in the block in 1387 mm during 1993 which is quite comparable with the district (1385 mm). Though this amount of rainfall is lower than the average normal rainfall in the State (1482 mm) it cannot be considered too low for cultivation. But the unevenness in rainfall is responsible for a low for a lower agricultural performance in lthe block. The monsoon period alone receives more than 80 per cent of total rainfall. Besides this uneven nature of rainfall, it is also found to be erratic. While in 1990 and 1991 the rainfall in the block was significantly more than the normal as well as actual rainfall in the State, however, in 1992 and 1993 the rainfall was much lower (Table 2.1). This unevenness and erratic nature of rainfall in the block is a main factor responsible for crop failure. Recently in 1996, the block had to face a severe drought due to the inadequate rainfall.

There are only three rivers, viz. Brutanga, Maluguni (previously known as Mandakini) and Sona, and a few springs flowing through the block, but these are small and seasonal. The ground-water potential under these river terrains is higher than any other places in the block. However, it could irrigate only a small portion of cultivated land if utilised fully.

Out of the total 31.03 thousand hectares of land in the block about 51 per cent is cultivated as against 44 per cent in the district and 41 per cent in the State (Table 2.2). of the rest, 6.7 per cent is under forests as against 14.52 per cent in the district and 35.25 per cent in the State. In addition, 4.8 per cent is barren and waste land, 18.65 per cent fallow land 4.59 per cent open grazing land and 8.95 per cent of the area comes under trees and groves. The share of fallow land and areas under trees and groves in the block are higher than that in the district and the State. A significant percentage of the area of trees and groves is covered under cashew orchards in the block. Considering the fact that only less than 10 per cent of the cultivated land is irrigated, the rest rainfed land is exposed to soil erosion during the major part of the year and hence, needs protection.

The problem of uneven endowment of land and water resources becomes more serious due to mismanagement of these resources over the years, resulting in environmental degradation. Due to deforestation land is degraded with the consequent erosion of soil.

Begunia does not have important mineral resources. However, it has some stone quarries in several parts of the block. It is considered as a great asset due to its use for house construction and labour absorption.

Sectoral Development

The acute poverty and backwardness can be traced to the backwardness of its agricultural and industrial sectors.

***(a) Agriculture*:** Agriculture is the main livelihood in the block. But the low level of irrigation and erratic rainfall has made the agriculture unstable and fluctuating. The most important constraining factor for the agricultural development in the block is the lack of sufficient irrigation facility. Eventhough it is located near the state capital, it is surprising to note that less than 10 per cent of the gross cropped area is irrigated as against more than 30 per cent in the State. The share of irrigated area in the block has increased marginally from 8.4 per cent in 1990-91 to 9.6 per cent in 1995-96.

There is not a single major or medium irrigation project in the (Table 2.3). This is contrast to the district, where about 66.52 per cent of the irrigation potential has been created by major and medium irrigation. Though some minor projects have been set up in the block the utilisation of the potential created is very low, i.e. less than 45 per cent. About 65 per cent of the total irrigated area comes through the traditional sources, viz., tanks and rivers (Table 2.4). The rest 35 cent of irrigation is made through dugwell and lift points.

Due to the lack of adequate irrigation, the cropping pattern in the block is not diversified. Foodgrains alone comprise near about 90 per cent of the total cultivated area, out of which the share of cereals is 62.59 per cent (Table 2.5). The shares of area under foodgrains and cereals are more than both the district as well as the State. Besides the area under foodgrains the share of vegetables in the block is about 8.36 per cent and this is more than that of the district and the State. However, the share of area covered under oilseeds in Begunia is significantly lower as compared to both the district and the State.

Eventhough the share of area under cereals in the block is more than that in the district, yet the productivity of paddy in the block is lower than that in the district (Table 2.6). The lower productivity in the block may be due to lack of adequate irrigation facility and the consequent use of small amount of fertiliser, at about 18.27 kg/ha in the block during 1995-96 as against 45.25 kg. per hectare in the district and 25.82 kg. per hectare at the State level.

Even if there is lack of sufficient irrigation in the block, about 22.61 per cent of the gross cropped area was covered under the high yielding varieties of crops in 1990-91, which increased to 33.22 per cent in 1995-96. The share of HYV to total gross cropped area is more pronounced in the southern region (23.81 per cent), followed by central region (22.95 per cent) in 1990-91. In North Begunia it is only 19.82 per cent. However, the use of modern implements for cultivation is not encouraging in the block. There are only 5 tractors, one power tiller, and 17 diesel pump sets in the block (Table 2.7). These are not adequate for agricultural development.

Besides the above agricultural backwardness, there is vast inequality in the distribution of land. The capitalist pattern of agriculture is reflected in the relatively large proposition of marginal land holders and agricultural labourers, and very small proportion of large land holders. While 67 per cent of marginal farmers hold only 8 per cent of agricultural land, only 8 per cnet of large farmers possess 33 per cnet of the total cultivated land (Table 2.8). All these indicate that the backwardness of agricultural sector in the block has the potential of creating more poverty land hunger.

(b) ***Industry:*** Industrial development in the Begunia block is far from satisfactory. There is not a single major and medium industry in the block. The number of small scale industry in the block is also very small. During 1992-93 there were noly 7 small scale industries in the block with the employment capacity of 44 persons (Table 2.9). The average capital investment per unit here is Rs. 106 thousand which is lower than both the district (Rs. 454 thousand) and the State (Rs. 260 thousand). However, the average employment of 6.29 persons is quite comparable with the district (6.40) as well as the State. There are only 2 forest based industries and one agro-based industry in the block. The employment in the forest based industry is significantly higher than other industries in the block (Table 2.10). Though there is more scope for agro-based industry in the block, which can absorb a significant number of workers, the government has not taken any step so far in that direction.

Besides the small scale industry, there are also cottage industries like handloom industries in the block. Though handlooms are widespread in the block, particularly in south Begunia it is not developed and modernised. Hence, lack of industrial development is responsible for the economic backwardness of the block, resulting in less employment for the poor. The reasons for low industrialisation might be due to the lack of entrepreneurship, lack of capital, lack of infrastructure and many others.

(c) ***Allied to Agriculture (Animal Husbandry):*** Begunia block has a sufficient number of bovine population. During 1995 (September) the total number of bovine population was 79.664 in the block, constituting 3983 per Gram Panchayat (Table 2.11). The share of cow is highest followed by bullock and then poultry bird. The

inhabitants of the block depend on these bovine population for their livelihood like milk, cultivation and meat. However, the extension service provided in the block for these bovine population is not satisfactory. Only one V.S., one additional V.S., 7 Livestock centres and 7 L.S. Inspectors, and 5 Insemination Centres are available in the Block. These are not adequate to meet the local needs.

Credit and Finance

For the agricultural developement Credit Co-operative Societies, Regional Rural Banks and Commercial Banks are operating in the Block. But due to the poor condition of the farmers and unstable agriculture they are unable to repay the loans brought from these cooperative societies. The overdue constitutes about 75 per cent of loan outstanding in credit Cooperative Societies and 50 per cent in Central Cooperative Societies by 1993 (Table 2.12). Such indebtedness indicates that poverty and hunger are wide spread in the Block.

Trade and Commerce

Since Begunia is situated on the State Highway and near to the business centres like Khurda, Nayagarh, Banki (Cuttack) and the State Capital, it has a vast scope for trade and business. While some merchandise products are exported, some are imported to the block. Goods are also traded within the block. Goods which are going out of the block for trade and business are cashew, handloom products, milk and milk products, vegetables, paddy, Mung, Biri, Sal Plate and Stone. On the other hand, goods which are entering into the Block for trade are consumer goods, cloth, grocery items, fist, egg, rice, vegetables etc. This shows that there is a vast potential for trade and commerce in the Block. But the lack of transportation facility in the block becomes a hindrance for the smooth functioning of the trade.

Employment Scenario

Absence of remunerative employment is the single most important factor responsible for poverty. Though all those unemployed are not poor, ensuring remunerative employment to the poor and hungry will go a long way towards alleviating hunger and poverty. It will, therefore, be useful to understand the main features of employment scene in the block and the changes that have been taken place.

Work force participation rate (WFPR) in the block is lower than that in the State (Table 2.13). This is also true in the case of both males and females. But while comparing the WFPR with the district it is found that female participation is more in the block than in the district.

Among the total main workers in the block the share of cultivator is highest followed by agricultural labourers. These two constitute more than 75 per cent of the total main workers in the block and are higher than the shares in the state (Table 2.14). However,the share of agricultural workers in the block has declined overtime from 1971 to 1991 and non-agricultural workers has increased significantly during the same period. This is also true in the case of the state but there the change is found to be marginal. The significant decline of agricultural workers is mostly due to the unstable agriculture. Within the non-farm sector, the percentage increase in the work force is more in the tertiary sector than in the secondary sector.

Human Resource Development

Literacy and health are two critical aspects of human resources development. These are also considered non-calorie indicators of poverty. Measurement of poverty on the basis of income/consumption levels tells us only a part of the story, as it does not give any information about the quality of life enjoyed by people-which is the ultimate goal of poverty alleviation. The performance of the block in the above two aspects of non-calorie indicators of poverty is presented below.

(a) ***Literacy:*** The general literacy in the block is found to be significantly higher that that in the State (Table 2.15). In both male and female literacy, its performance is better than the state, though it is not better than the district. However, this does not indicate that the quality of life in respect of literacy is better among the poor and the vulnerable sections. The literacy rate is much lower for the S.C. and S.T. The share of S.C./S.T. students (5.77 per cent) in the block is also lower than their share of population (21.0 per cent). This is the direct result of the failure to promote universal primary education.

However, after the introduction of mid-day meal scheme the attendance in school has improved only for food and not for anything else. This will not improve the quality of life.

(b) ***Health:*** The major variable considered in health is infant mortality rate (IMR). Though there is reduction in the IMR, yet the position of the block compared to the district and the state continues to be disappointing (Table 2.16). During 1995-96 the IMR in Begunia Block was 113 as against 103 in the district and the state. The reduction in the IMR in the block is significant lower than that in the State, though it is higher than the district.

The lower performance of IMR is observed inspite of better health infrastructure in the block. The infrastructure facilities such as number of health centres, doctors, beds for patients etc.have also increased within a period of 5 years from 1991-92 to 1995-96 (Table 2.17). But the mere infrastructure facility does not help the improvement in health care. Due to the irregular attendance of the doctors in the hospital and free supply of medicines only in communicable diseases, the poor and needy patients have to find the alternative. It is also strange to note that there is no ICDS and Anganwadi Centres in the block.

(c) ***Drinking Water:*** The drinking water facility in the block is better than that in the district. About 97.47 per cent of the villages have water facility in the block as compared to 94.52 per cent in the district. Though Table 2.18 presents a rosy picture of infrastructure for drinking water, a significant proportion of tubewells and to some extent wells are not functioning properly and no care is being taken to imrove the position. Disinfectants are also rarely used in the open wells. It is, therefore, required that the authorities should take more interest to provide safe drinking water in the block.

Infrastructure Development

(a) ***Roads:*** A significant development has been made in respect of roads in the Block. Most of the villages are well connected with all weather *kutcha* roads (though *pucca* to some extent) and are motorable. The road length per one thousand population in the block is 4.03 km (1996-97) as against 5.68 km (1988-89) in Orissa.

Eventhough the road length in the block is comparable with that in the state, transportation facility is not provided to all the Panchayats in the Block. This severely hampers the trade and business carried out in the Block.

(b) Electricity: About 99 per cent of the villages in the block are electrified as against 92 per cent in the district and 70 per cent in the State. But the supply is not regular. Whereas the central region is assumed of regular supply of electricity, the southern and northern regions are affected by irregular supply. Besides there is a great deal of misuse of electricity. Therefore, the mere availability of electricity can not help the poor in the block. Public interventions are needed to supply electricity to all the houses interested for the same. There is also the need for preventing misuse of electricity through active government intervention.

Migration

Due to backwardness of agriculture and industry, there is lack of ample employment opportunities in the block.This makes people to migrate to distant places like Surat, Delhi, Madhya Pradesh, Calcutta and other places in search of availing employment. Hence, migration plays an important role in the Begunia block for livelihood.

Regional Disparities

Before we proceed to discuss the extent of hunger and poverty we should see whether the block is homogenous with regard to the resources and growth pattern. Within the three regions in the block, namely, central, north and south, the following differences are observed.

Locationally central Begunia has more advantage as compared to north or the south Begunia. While block headquarter is situated in central Begunia, south Begunia and north Begunia are away from the block headquarter, with the former far away as compared to the latter.

The proportion of Net Sown Area in south region is lower than both north and central regions. South Begunia has also lower proportion of irrigated area and forest area. But contrary to this, south

Begunia has higher proportion of area under trees and groves, grazing land and fallow land. Most of cashew orchards are found in south Begunia. A significant proportion of land is put to non-agricultural use in south Begunia as compared to north and central Begunia (Table 2.19).

South Begunia is equipped with cottage industry like handloom which is absent in north or central begunia. Besides this, stone quarries are found in south and central Begunia, with the higher proportion in south than central Begunia.

Educational facilities as well as health facilities are found to be better in south Begunia than both central and north Begunia. This is reflected by their higher proportion of infrastructural facilities like schools, health centres, beds for patients etc. The proportion of bovine population, particularly cow, goat and poultry birds in south Begunia is higher compared to either the north or the central.

Eventhough south Begunia has fair weather roads to all panchayats and are motorable, there is lack of sufficient transport facility. Since it is far away from the block headquarter, the lack of proper transportation hampers the trade and business activities to a great extent.

Hence, though significant dfference is not observed in the resources and development activities in these regions, heterogeneity is observed to some extent in the above respects.

Extent of Poverty and Hunger

Due to the above socio-economic backwardness of the block the incidence of poverty is observed to be severe. According to the 1992 survey conducted by the block about 83.0 per cent of the total households in the block remained below the poverty line. This is significantly higher than the district figure (75.9 per cent). The severiety is more in the case of S.C. and S.T. households; the share of S.C/S.T. households in total households under below poverty line significantly higher than their population share (Table 2.20).

Not only the households below poverty line are significant in the block, but also the poorest of the poor, whose income remained below Rs.6000/- per annum are significantly more, representing about

78.0 per cent of the total poor people who remained below the poverty line (Table 2.21). This shows that there is extreme poverty and hunger in the block. This significantly higher level of poverty and hunger is due to the poor socio-economic background of the block, on the one hand and lack of proper policy and its effective implementation, on the other.

Government Interventions

In order to alleviate poverty and hunger the government has been implementing various programmes and measures in the Begunia block since its inception in 1961. But still the extent of poverty and hunger has been increasing. The programme which are now being implemented in the block and have direct or indirect attack on poverty land hungry are; Integrated Rural Developemnt Programme (IRDP), Training of Rural Youth for Self-Employment (TRYSEM), Development of Women and Children in Rural Areas (DWCRA), Million Wells Scheme (MWS), Jawahar Rojagar Yojana (JRY), Indira Awas Yojana(IAY). Old Age Pension (OAP), Fish Farmers' Development Agency (FFDA), S.C. & S.T. Developement Finance Cooperative Corporation (DFCC), Public Distribution System (PDS), Operation Black Board (OBB) and Improvemment Tool Kits etc. But the programmes have not yielded significant results as have been discussed in a separate chapter.

Table 2.1

Rainfall in Begunia and Orissa

(In mm)

Year	*Begunia*	*Orissa*
1990	1906	1865.8
1991	1713	1462.2
1992	1099	1344.1
1993	1387	1415.9

Note: Normal Rainfall in Orissa is 1482.2 mm.

Source: Office of the Begunia Block, and Directorate of Agriculture and Food Production, Government of Orissa.

Table 2.2

Land Utilisation Pattern During 1992-93

(In hectares)

		Begunia	*Khurda*	*Orissa (000'Ha)*
1.	Forest	2,074 (6.68)	37,751 (14.52)	326 (32.25)
2.	Tress & Groves	2,777 (8.95)	17,426 (6.70)	26 (5.51)
3.	Net Sown Area	15,786 (50.87)	1,14,979 (44.23)	457 (40.80)
4.	Fallow Land	5,788 (18.65)	22,520 (8.66)	25 (2.49)
5.	Land for Non-Agril use	1,691 (5.45)	25,303 (9.73)	67 (5.03)
6.	Grazing Land	1,425 (4.59)	12,378 (4.76)	67 (4.27)
7.	Uncultivable Land	406 (1.31)	15,457 (5.95)	43 (3.42)
8.	Cultivable Waste	1,084 (3.49)	14,130 (5.44)	37 (3.46)
9..	Total Geographical Area	31,031 (100.00)	2,59,944 (100.00)	1,046 (100.00)

Note: Figures in Parentheses are percentage share of total area.

Source: Government of Orissa, Directorate of Economics & Statistics, District Statistical Handbook of Khurda, 1993.

Table 2.3

Irrigation Potential Created During 1992-93

(In 000' Ha)

		Begunia	Khurda
1.	Major & Medium		83.217 (66.52)
2.	Minor Flow	1.744 (33.68)	11.969 (9.57)
3.	Lift	1.143 (22.07)	6.634 (5.30)
4.	Others	2.291 (44.24)	23.282 (18.61)
5.	Total	5.178 (100.00)	125.10 (100.00)

Note: Figures in parentheses are percentage share of total.
Source: Government of Orissa, Directorate of Economics & Statistics, District Statistical Handbook, Bhubaneswar, 1993.

Table 2.4

Source-wise Area Irrigated in Begunia Block

(In Hectare)

		1990-91	*1995-96*
1.	Minor Canel & Tanks	602 (30.04)	775 (33.92)
2.	Rivers	707 (35.21)	707 (30.94)
3.	Lift Irrigation Points	400 (19.96)	450 (19.69)
4.	Dugwells	295 (14.72)	353 (15.54)
5.	Totals	2004 (100.00)	2285 (100.00)
	Share of irrigated area in total cropped area (in%)	8.40	9.60

Note: Figures in parentheses are percentage share of total irrigated area.
Source: Ofifce of the Agricultural Extension Officer, Begunia.

Table 2.5

Cropping Pattern During 1995-96

(Area in Hectare)

	Begunia	*Khurda (000'Ha)*	*Orissa (000'Ha)*
Food Crope	21306 (89.49)	184.3 (87.39)	7194.0 (78.20)
(a) Cereals	14901 (62.59)	119.5 (56.67)	5015.5 (54.52)
(b) Pulses	6405 (26.90)	64.8 (30.72)	2178.5 (23.68)
Other Crops	2501 (10.51)	26.6 (12.61)	2005.6 (21.80)
(a) Oilseeds	403 (1.69)	7.9 (3.75)	1146.7 (12.46)
(b) Vegetables	1991 (8.36)	16.9 (8.01)	744.7 (8.09)
(c) Others	107 (0.45)	1.8 (0.85)	114.2 (1.25)
Total Crops	23807 (100.00)	210.90 (100.00)	9199.60 (100.00)

Note: Figures in bracktes are percentage share of total areas.
Source: Office of the Agricultural Extension Officer, Begunia and Directorate of Economics and Statistics, Government of Orissa, Bhubaneswar.

Table 2.6

Area, Production and Yield of Paddy Crops in 1993

	Begunia	*Khurda*
Area (in Ha)	15867	128660
Production (in Qt.)	223834	2116327
Yield (Qt/Ha)	21.37	24.92

Source: Government of Orissa, Directorate of Economics & Statistics, District Statistical Handbook, Khurda (1993), Bhubaneswar, 1994.

Table 2.7

Agricultural Implements Used in the Block by September 1995

SL. No.	Items	*Central*	*North*	*South*	*Block* Total
1.	Plough	2924 (18.34)	4456 (27.94)	8566 (53.72)	15946 (100.00)
2.	Mai/Leveller	1750 (29.02)	756 (12.54)	3534 (58.61)	6030 (100.00)
3.	Bullock Cart	932 (22.34)	985 (23.62)	2254 (54.04)	4171 (100.00)
4.	Diesel Pump Set	06 (35.29)	1 (5.88)	10 (58.82)	17 (100.00)
5.	Tractor	05 (100.00)	0 (0.00)	0 (0.00)	5 (100.00)
6.	Power Tiller	01 (100.00)	0 (0.00)	0 (0.00)	1 (100.00)
	Total	5618 (21.47)	619/8 (23.68)	14364 (54.89)	26170 (100.00)

Note: Figures in the parentheses are percentage share of total block.
Source: Office of the Veterinary Officer, Begunia.

Table 2.8

Percentage Share of Different Category of Farmers inTotal Number of Farmers in Different Regions & Begunia Block During 1991

Region	*Marginal Farmer*	*Small Farmer*	*Large Farmer*	*Total Farmer*
Central	65.42 (7.31)	27.09 (62.20)	7.49 (30.49)	100.00 (100.00)
North	66.76 (8.89)	25.68 (60.93)	7.56 (30.18)	100.00 (100.00)
South	68.87 (8.04)	23.64 (55.99)	8.49 (35.97)	100.00 (100.00)
Block	67.07 (8.08)	24.89 (58.58)	8.04 (33.34)	100.00 (100.00)

Note: Figures in the parentheses are percentage share of total area operated by different category of farmers.
Source: Office of the Agricultural Extension Officer, Begunia.

Table 2.9

Number of SSI Units, capital Invested and Employment During 1992-93

	Begunia	Khurda	Orissa
No. of Units	7	172	2117
Capital Invested (Rs. in '000)	741	78167	549996
C.I. Per Unit (Rs.thousand)	105.86	454.46	259.80
Person Employed	44	1114	13344
Person Employed Per Unit	6.29	6.48	6.30

Source: Government of Orissa, Directorate of economics & Statistics, District Statistical Handbook, Khurda, (1993).
Government of Orissa, DE&S, Economic Survey, Orissa (1996-97).

Table 2.10

Number of SSI Units, Capital Invested and Persons Employed in Different Types of Industries in Begunia Block and Khurda District During 1992-93

SL. No.	Types of Industry	Begunia			Khurda		
		No. of Units	*Capital Invested (in '000)*	*Persons Employed*	*No. of Units*	*Capital Invested (in '000)*	*Personal Employed*
1.	Food & Allied	1	115	2	25	41315	192
2.	Chemical & Allied	--	-	--	5	726	24
3.	Electrical & Electronics	--	--	--	11	1686	72
4.	Engineering & Metal Based	1	65	2	25	3193	157
5.	Forest & Wood Product	2	208	25	13	1744	94
6.	Glass & Ceramic	1	62	5	12	10989	207
7.	Textiles	1	56	5	11	1471	100
8.	Miscellaneous	1	235	5	36	6746	116
9.	Repairing	--	--	--	20	5109	82
10.	Paper & Paper Product	--	--	--	9	2648	40
11.	Total	07	741	44	167	75627	1084

Source: Government of Orissa, Directorate of Economics & Statistics, District Statistical Handbook, Khurda (1993), Bhubaneswar.

Table 2.11

Distribution of Bovine Population id Different Region of Begunia Block During September, 1995

(In Nos.)

Sl. No.	*Items*	*Central Region*	*North Region*	*South Region*
1.	Cow	5,236	6,338	14,117
2.	Bullock	3,658	7,509	11,340
3.	Male-Buffalow	36	209	375
4.	Female-Buffalow	---	02	262
5.	Goat	332	2,096	3,494
6.	Sheep	1,677	3,427	3,335
7.	Poultry Birds	2,198	3,926	8,505
8.	Total Bovine	13,137	23,507	41,428

Source: Office of the Veterinary Officer, Begunia.

Table 2.12

Performance of Cooperative Societies in respect of their Loan Advancement in Begunia Block and Khurda District During 1993.

		Agricultural Cooperative Credit Society		*Central Cooperative Society*	
		Begunia	*Khurda*	*Begunia*	*Khurda*
1.	No.	15	154	1	8
2.	Loan Advanced	2908	---	2763	39165
3.	Overdue (in '000)	2556	29235	2153	36794
4.	Loan Outstanding	3321	36261	4299	71945
5.	Overdue as % loan outstanding	76.96	80.62	50.08	51.14

Source: Government of Orissa, directorate of economics & Sta tistics, District Statistical handbook, 1993.

Table 2.13

Work Participation Rate in 1991

(In Percentage)

	1991		
	MALE	*FEMALE*	*TOTAL*
Begunia	50.28	7.74	29.19
Khurda	50.50	7.16	29.94
Orissa	53.74	20.85	37.53

Source: Government of India, Primary Census Abstruct, Cen sus of India, 1991.

Table 2.14

Distribution of Workers in Begunia and Orissa During 1971 and 1991

(In Percentage)

Workers	*Begunia*		*Orissa*	
	1971	*1991*	*1971*	*1991*
Cultivators	48.22	43.45	49.16	44.21
Agricultural Labourers	36.07	32.02	28.28	28.85
Livestock etc.	0.94	1.16	--	--
Mining & Manufacturing	5.54	8.33	3.63	3.47
Construction, Trade and Transport	2.36	7.48	--	--
Others	6.89	7.56	18.93	23.47
Total	100.00	100.00	100.00	100.00

Source: Government of India, Primary Census Abstract, Census of India, 1971 and 1991.

Table 2.15

Literacy Rate in Begunia, Khurda and Orissa During 1991

(In Percentage)

	Begunia	*Khurda*	*Orissa*
Total	63.58	67.72	49.09
Male	76.74	78.74	63.09
Female	50.36	55.39	34.68

Source: Government of India, Census of India, 1991.

Table 2.16

Infant Mortality Rate

(Per Thousand Live Birth)

AREA	*1992-93*	*1995-96*
BEGUNIA	120	113
KHURDA	110	103
ORISSA	124	103

Source: Office of C.D.M.O., Khurda.

Table 3.17

Health Infrastructure in Begunia Block

ITEMS	*1991-92*	*1995-96*
No. of C.H.C	1	1
N o. of Additional PHC/PHC (N)	7	10
No. of Dispensaries	19	19
No. of Doctors	11	13
No. of Beds	24	24
No. of Nurses & Midwives	9	26
No. of Homeopathic Dispensary	1	1

Source: Office of the C.H.C., Botalma, Begunia Block

Table 2.18

Region-wise Facilities of Drinking Water in Begunia Block

Area	*Tubewell*	*Wells*
CENTRAL	85	95
NORTH	94	101
SOUTH	297	300
TOTAL	476	496

Source: Office of Different GPs, Begunia Block.

Table 2.19

Region-wise land Utilisation Pattern in Begunia Block During 1991

(In Percentage)

ITEMS	*CENTRAL*	*NORTH*	*SOUTH*	*BLOCK*
Forst	3.90	1.69	1.48	2.15
Trees & Groves	4.73	5.24	5.92	5.45
Net Sown Area	58.80	60.30	56.74	58.17
Fallow Land	3.34	2.42	4.83	4.10
Land for Non-Agril. Use	11.36	8.97	13.63	11.87
Grazing Land	6.17	7.64	8.72	7.80
Barren Land	6.81	7.95	6.80	7.09
Waste Land	4.89	4.79	1.88	3.38
Total Geographical Area	100.00	100.00	100.00	100.00
Gross Cropped Area (in Ha)	7406.40	7445.66	14452.94	29305.00
Irrigated area (As % of GCA)	9.78	8.47	7.78	8.40

Source: Office of the Agricultural Extension Officers, Begunia and Gadamanitri, Begunia Block.

Table 2.20

Below Poverty Line (BPL) Families in Begunia and Khurda During 1992

ITEMS	*BEGUNIA*	*KHURDA*
Total No. of Rural Family	19051	183715
No. of BPL (1992)	15736	139453
BPL as % of total Rural Famly	82.60	75.91
Share of BPL Population (%)		
S.C	11.71	16.87
S.T.	18.58	6.74
O.C.	69.71	76.39

Source: Government of Orissa, Directorate of Economics & Statistics, District Statistical Handbook, Khurda 1993.

Table 2.21

Distribution of BPL Families in 1992

(In Percentage)

Income Group Distribution	*Begunia*	*Khurda*
Upto 4000	29.28	27.90
4001-6000	48.93	46.20
6001-8500	16.49	18.60
8500-11,000	5.31	7.31

Source: Government of Orissa, Directorate of Economics & Statistics, District Statistical Handbook, Khurda, 1993.

ANNEXURE -I

List of Panchayats and Revenue Villages Under Different Regions of the Block

Region	*Name of the Panchayats*	*Name of the Villages*
Central	1. Begunia	Begunia, Jagiribada, Odagaon, Balabhadrapur, Jaganathpur, Balarampur, Bhipur, Golapatna, Kushupala.
	2. Radhakanta pur	Kalikaprasad, Radhakantapur, Chakapada, Gadataura, Durgapur, Khamardhip, Mohanpur, Parvatipur, Chandiprasad, Laxmiprasad, Hariprasad, Suanal, Dhanaghar, Nuagaon.
	3. Saura	Sarua, Lokanathpur, Patanibar, Swapneswarpur, Katha, Khuntia
	4. Baghamari	Baghamari, Pariketa (b), Panashabasta, Aatree, Bamadiha, Saradhapur, Kuranga (B).
North	1. Podadiha	Podadiha, Ostapur, Kotapalla, Barasahi, Podadiha Patna, Paikara Sahi, Talagada, Diniary, Nilakanthapur, Sana Tulashipur, Bada Tulashipur.
	2. Kantabada	Kantabada, Tandala, Jemabanta, Mukundapur, Basudevpur, Malli Padar, Kendupalli.
	3. Badaberana	Badaberana, Govindapur, Kuluhapatna, Narasinghpur, Basudevpur, aheswarpur, Darudhipa (B).
	4.Simor	Simor, Chanpatisahi, Hatasahi, Simor Patna, Gaonpur, Kantamalima.

Region	*Name of the Panchayats*	*Name of the Villages*
	5. Pangarasingh	Pangarsingh, Bhogada, Paikasahi, Lekhanpur, Samantarpur, Kuradhilo, Godipokhari, Taramaru.
	1. Dinger	Dinger, Parsurampur, Chandiapalla, Bhuansunipatna, Chodapalanga, Lehanga.
	2. Routpada	Routpada, Hemantapurpatna, Dakshneswar, Thanpalli, Uttereswar, Kotalanga.
South	3.Bottalama	Bottalama, Hirapur, Raimulpatna, Raimul, Manikapurpatna, Badabarabati, Goudapatna, Khuntabandha, Dova, Jallavara, Chhatrapada, Indupur, Goudiapada, Atharanga, Akhupadar.
	4. Hajja	Hajja, Narogoda, Kollarajhar, Bala Jhati, Nidhipur, Muktapur.
	5. Siko	Siko, Khadipadar, Borigaon, Chandrasekharpur, Ekdalia, Belapada.
	6. Sagadabhanga	Sagadabhanga, Godikilo, Radhamohanpur, Betarjanga.
	7.Godamanitri	Nandapurpatna, Chhima, Lakhapada, Manapur.
	8. Durgapur	Durgapur, Karadagadia, Gokulpur, Narasinghpur, Jagannathpur, Botalama, Ramsinghprasad, Lalitadeipur, Nilakantapur, Bengitangi, Kesarda,.Sikharada, Fala Chhanchuni (B).

Region	*Name of the Panchayats*	*Name of the Villages*
	9.Govindapur	Govindpur, Gopalpur, Berhampurpatna, Berhampur, Lokipur.
	10. Deuli	Deuli, Gopinathpur, Ogalpur, Kuruma, Dangapada, Samantarpur, Goda, Dalaka, Parichhala, Kalikaprasad.
	11. Kunjuri	Kunjuri, Dalatola, Kunjabiharipatna, Nianmunha, Patimalla, Srirampur, Chhania, Baragoda, Balipatna, Godi, Godisahi, Bhatapada, Kokasingh, Patna, Balipatna, Chandi, Mansania.

Note: B tends for 'Bechhapari' (Inhabitants).
Source: Office of the Begunia Block.

3

Methodology

In order to alleviate poverty and hunger different programmes have been implemented in the State of Orissa since the inception of the planning period. The strategy for the removal of poverty has undergone frequent changes; starting from community development programme i.e. area based approach to the target group approach. But still after 50 years of planning there is prevalence of transitory poverty along with chronic poverty in some underdeveloped blocks, which leads to hunger, starvation, misery and in some cases distress migration. People in these blocks have suffered mainly due to constant neglect, multiple deprivation and exploitation through agencies of outside traders, local feudal elements, power brokers and the state bureaucracy. The programmes implemented in these areas are often not integrated with the development needs or resource base of the area. Hence, there is a need for extensive and comprehensive study to know the causes of problems, particularly of hunger, starvation and poverty and to find out the permanent solution of the problem. With this background, an attempt is made here to study lthe causes of poverty and hunger and its solution in Begunia, an underdeveloped block of Orissa.

Issues Involved

The main issues raised in this study are

(i) Do the public intervention in the sphere of access to land and water, assets development, institutional credit, employ ment, minimum real wage, and basic needs help in eradication of poverty in rural areas?

(ii) Whether the poor remains hungry amidst different poverty alleviation programmes?

(iii) Is it possible to empower the rural mass through decentral isation of power at village level or right to information of the people of various programmes and their implementat-ion, which may help to eradicate poverty?

(iv) Is the public investment in human resource developemnt an instrument to improve the lot of the people by improving their skill and increasing their access to information which ultimately help them in both rural farm and non-farm sect-ors?

Objectives of the Study

The main objectives of this study are

(i) To study the extent of hunger in the block.

(ii) To study the measures and programmes which are being implemented by the Government in the block in order to remove hunger.

(iii) To identify the critical gaps and missing links of the exist-ing programmes and assess the measure taken to cover it.

(iv) To identify lthe catalysts for growth in the block and fixat-ion of priority of investment.

(v) To study some specific areas which are necessary for the overall development of the block.

Methodological Issues

The present study tries to adopt a methodology, which forms a vital part of any economic investigation. Attempt has been made here to describe the sample design, the measurement of the effect of poverty alleviation programmes, sources and methods of data collection and the statistical methods and tools used in the present study.

The Sample Design

Simple random sampling method has been used to study the impact of different poverty alleviation programmes implemented in the block. The study is based on the data collected from the beneficiaries of different programmes spread over different Gram Panchayats in the Begunia block. The selection of different poverty alleviation programmes (PAPS), Gram Panchayats (GPS), Villages and households are presented in the following.

Selection of Poverty Alleviation Programmes

Since one of the main objectives of the study is to evaluate different programmes which are working in the block to alleviate poverty and hunger, we have selected all the programmes which are linked with poverty and hunger. For the purpose of the study we have selected the following poverty alleviation programmes: Integrated Rural Development Programme (IRDP), Training of Rural Youth for Self Employment (TRYSEM), Development of Women and Children in Rural Area (DWCRA), Fish Farmers Development Agency (FFDA), Scheduled Caste and Scheduled Tribe Development Finance Cooperative (DFCC) Jawahar Rojagar Yojana (JRY), Million W--ells Scheme (MWS), Indira Awas Yojana (IAY), Old Age Pension (OAP) or Widow Pension (WP) and Public Distribution System (PDS).

The programmes like IRDP, TRYSEM, DWCRA, FFDA and DFCC are meant for self-employment and entrepreneurship development while the programmes like JRY, is for wage employment, and MWS and IAY for infrastructure development.OAP is a income transfer scheme, while PDS is a scheme which is meant to distribute foodgrains and some other essential commodities at lower than market prices. These programmes can be categorised into three groups: (i) Direct attack on poverty target groups, (ii) Direct Income transfer, and (iii) Indirect income subsidisation. All the above mentioned programmes come under the first group with the exception of OAP and PDS which come under second and third groups respectively. Among the direct poverty alleviation programmes, the important ones are IRDP, TRYSEM, DWCRA, JRY & MWS. Schemes like FFDA and DFCC are not wide spread in the block and are of less importance.

Selection of GPs and Villages

As per the guidelines provided by the P.R. Department, Government of Orissa, our study covers all the 20 Gram Panchayats (GPs) in the Begunia block. Out of the 20 GPs, 4 are centrally located, 5 are situated in the north and the rest 11 are located in the south.

The selection of villages is based on their concentration of SC & ST population. From each Gram Panchayat one village is selected on the basis of its highest concentration of SC/ST population. However, it is required that the selected villages should have adequate number of beneficiaries during the period under study. In the absence of it in some cases we have switched over to the next alternate village for our study. The selected villages from each Panchayat are presented in Table 3.1.

Selection of Beneficiaries

The beneficiaries is each village have been selected by using the random sampling method. However, the number of beneficiaries in each village is restricted to 10 and the beneficiaries in different programmes are drawn on the basis of the share of their total beneficiaries in the village. This ensures that the samples draw are in proportion to the share of beneficiaries in different programmes.

The beneficiaries are spread over the period from 1991-92 to 1993-94. However, the programmes like DWCRA has been implemented since 1994-95 and hence, the study period is relaxed in this case. The list of the beneficiaries is collected from the Block Office. The total number of beneficiaries selected for the survey are 200. The sample beneficiaries are distributed according to their strength in the block as a whole. While the number of sample beneficaries covered under the self-employment programmes is 121; the numbers of sample beneficiaries under wage employment, infrastructure development and income transfer programmes are 23,34 and 22 respectively. The distribution of beneficiaries under different programmes is presented in Table 3.1.

Besides the survey of beneficiaries, we have also surveyed 40 non-beneficiaries, 2 from each selected village, as control sample. The income, expenditure, asset position, debt and other relevant variables of the beneficiaries are compared with the non- beneficiaries.

Questionnaire and its Coverage

The relevant information of both beneficiaries and non-beneficiaries are collected with the help of a detailed questionnaire. Since the basic objectives of most programmes are to generate additional income and employment so as to reduce the extent and intensity of poverty, attempts have been made to assess the income and employment generated by different programmes before and after the assistance. It may be pointed out that the income and employment estimates arrived at through the said questionnaire are only close approximations because it is not possible to get the accurate data due to several limitations. The income of the cultivators in our study is Farm Business Income and has been worked out by subtracting only actual money cost incurred from the gross value of output.

Measurement of Additional Income and Employment

The generation of additional income and employment can be measured by either of the two approaches: (i) Before-After (BA) Approach and (ii) with -without (WW) Approach, where before and without serving as the control. In the BA approach, the present condition of the beneficiaries is compared with the condition before assistance. On the other hand, in the WW approach, the present condition of the beneficiaries is compared with the present condition of the non-beneficiaries. In the present study, we have used the BA approach to assess the impact of poverty alleviation programmes on the generation of income and employment. However, to assess the impact on the socio-economic condition of the beneficiaries we have used the WW approach.

To measure the additional income in the BA approach, the present income of the beneficiaries is compared with the income at the time of assistance. In this case, the annual income of the beneficiaries is measured at constant prices. For deflating the present income we have used the consumer price index of the agricultural labourers in Orissa as is seen the Economic Survey of Orissa (1996-97). To maintain the homogeneity in the income of the beneficiaries before assistance, income at the time of assistance is also measured at the 1991-92 prices.

To measure the additional employment in the BA approach no such adjustrment is necessary. Here one manday work is considered equivalent to 8 working hours. But the data are rough approximations and may not be accurate as most of the beneficiaries from whom these data are collected cannot maintain any such records.

Sources and Method of Data Collection

The data for this study have been collected from both Primary and secondary sources. The primary data are collected by personally interviewing 240 households inhabitating in 20 villages of Begunia block here the household is taken as the unit. Out of the 240 households, 200 are beneficiary households and rest 40 are non-beneficiary households. The relevant informations from both beneficiary and non-beneficiary households are collected with the help of specially designed schedules as mentioned above. We have collected the necessary informations of the households for the year 1995-96 and at the time of assistance. Since 1996-97 is not a normal year, we have avoided collecting data for the said year though we have collected data like PDS and some others for that year. It should be pointed out that the data so collected are based on the memory of the respondents and are only close approximations.

The secondary data are collected from various published and unpublished sources, such as frem the Secretariat; Directorate of Economics & Statistics, Orissa; Begunia Block; Office of the Agricultural Extension Officers, Directorate of Health, Education, etc.

Statistical Methods Used

The basic objective of different programmes used in this study is to alleviate poverty, i.e. to reduce the extent and intencity of poverty among the beneficiaries. To measure the extent and intensity of poverty we have used simple statistical tools, such as mean, mode and coefficient of variation.

Reduction in the extent of povery can be measured by finding out the percentage of beneficiaries crossing the poverty line after assistance. But this meeasure the reduction in the intensity of poverty. If the income of the beneficiaries increases after assistance but is not sufficient enough to cross the poverty line, the intensity of poverty is reduced although not the extent of poverty. This is due to vertical movement of the beneficiaries along the higher income classes.

We have used the following methods for the measurement of reducrtion in the intensity of poverty:

(a) If the modal class of the income distribution among the benefactaries remains the same with lower frequency or shifts to the higher income brackets and in general there is movement of the beneficiaries from the lower to the higher income brackets, the intensity of the poverty of the beneficiaries can be said to have been reduced.

(b) An increase in mean income of the beneficiaries simultaneo usly with a decrease or no change in the coefficient of varia tion implies a reduction in tintensity of poverty for the benefici aries having an income less than the average income of the beneficiaries as a whole (i.e. for the poorest among the poor). On the other hand, an increase in mean income accompanied by the increase in the coefficient of variation implies a reduct ion in intensity of poverty for the beneficiaries belonging to higher income brackets among the beneficiaries.

Table 3.1

Distribution of Sample Beneficiaries of Different Programmes in theSeclected Villages.

Sl. No.	*Gram Panchayat*	*Village*	*Selfemployment Programme*			
			IRDP	*TRYSEM*	*DWCRA*	*FFDA*
1	2	3	4	5	6	7
	Central					
1.	Begunia	Kusapalla	8	-	-	-
2	Radhakantapur	Radhakantapur	-	-	6	-
3.	Sarua	Saru	8	-	-	-
4.	Baghamari	Baghamari	5	-	2	-
	North					
5.	Podadiha	Nilakanthapur	5	2	-	-
6.	Kantabada	Jemabantadei	2	4	-	-
7.	Badaberana	Govindapur	3	2	-	1
8.	Simor	Simorpatna	4	-	-	-
9.	Pongarsingh	Kuradhilo	2	-	-	-
	South					
10.	Dingar	Chhotipalanga	-	-	-	-
11.	Routpada	Dakshineswar	7	-	-	-
12.	Botalma	Hirapur	1	-	-	-
13	Haza	Haza	3	1	3	-
14.	Siko	Siko	6	-	-	-
15	Sagadabhanga	Sagadabhanga	8	-	-	-
16.	Gadamanitri	Gadamanitri	3	2	3	-
17.	Durgapur	Managovindpur	7	-	-	-
18.	Govindpur	Gopalpur	5	1	-	-
19.	Deuli	Samantarapur	7	-	-	-
20	Kunjuri	Kunjuri	6	-	-	-
21.	All		90 (45.00)	12 (6.00)	14 (700)	1 (0.50)

Table 3.1 (contd...)

Self Employment Programmes Contd.			*Wage Emp-Loyment Programme*	*Infrastructure Development Programme*			*Transfer earning Programmes*	*Total*
Sl. No.	*DECC*	*TOTAL*	*JRY*	*MWS*	*IAY*	*TOTAL*	*OAP*	
1	8	9	10	11	12	13	14	15
1.	-	8	-	1	-	1	1	10
2.	-	6	-	3	-	3	1	10
3.	-	8	-	1	-	1	1	10
4.	-	7	1	1	-	1	1	10
5	-	7	1	-	-	-	2	10.
6.	-	6	1	-	2	2	1	10
7.	-	6	2	1	1	2	-	10
8.	-	4	3	-	-	-	3	10
9.	-	2	2	5	-	5	1	10
10.	4	4	2	3	-	3	1	10
11.	-	7	-	2	-	2	1	10
12.	-	1	2	6	-	6	1	10
13.	-	7	1	1	-	1	1	10
14.	-	6	2	2	-	2	-	10
15.	-	8	-	1	-	1	1	10
16.	-	8	1	-	-	-	1	10
17.	-	7	2	-	-	-	1	10
18.	-	6	1	2	-	-	1	10
19.	-	7	-	2	-	-	1	10
20.	-	6	2	-	-	-	2	10
21.	4	121	23	31	3	34	22	200
	(2.00)	(60.50)	(11.50)	(15.50)	(1.50)	(17.00)	(11.00)	(100.00)

Note: Figures in the parentheses are percentage of total.
Source: Data compiled from Field Survey.

4

Measures and Programmes Adopted by the Government for the Target Groups and Their Achievement

This Chapter is divided into two parts. In the first part different measures and programmes adopted by the Government for the target groups are studied, while in the second part critical gaps and missing links are identified.

PART-I

GOVERNMENT ACTION AGAINST POVERTY AND HUNGER

The State Government has taken many measures for alleviating poverty and hunger in the Begunia block. The programmes which are now being implemented in the block have been divided into the following three groups:

(A) Asset Creation and Rural Employment Programmes:

(a) Self-Employment Programmes.

(b) Wage Employment Programmes.

(c) Infrastructure Development Programmes.

(B) Social Security Programmes

(C) Food Security Programmes

A review of the performance of these programmes in alleviating poverty and hunger in Begunia Block is presented in the following:

(A) ASSET CREATION AND RURAL EMPLOYMENT PROGRAMMES

(a) Self-Employment Programmes

1. Integrated Rural Development Programme(IRDP)

IRDP, introduced in the year 1978-79,is the most important poverty alleviation programme in the State of Orissa. It was extended to all blocks in the country from 2nd October 1980. However, it was launched in the Begunia Block during 1978-79. The main objective of the programme is to assist the families below the poverty line in rural areas to cross the poverty line by taking up self-employment ventures. It is a credit linked programme. It has three dimensions: Income Generation, Employment Generation and the Target Group Approach.

Targets and Achievements: The financial allocations and fixation of targets for assisting families are based on the incidence of poverty. Data pertaining to year-wise physical target of beneficiaries and their achievements in Begunia Block and in Orissa over a period of five years are presented in Table1. While the number of beneficiaries assisted under the programme exceeded the targets fixed in different years in the state as a whole, it is not so in Begunia block. While the achievement is more than the target in some years, it falls short in 1994-95 (Table 4.1). The short fall of target reflects the inefficiency on the part of the government in implementing the programme. During the year 1994-95, the financial share of the block in the state total matches approximately the share of target for the beneficiaries. This is in contrast to other years, where the share of target exceeded the share of financial allocation (Table 4.2).

The proportion of subsidy has remained more or less unchanged from 1991-92 to 1993-94, and increased significantly in 1994-95 (Table 4.3). This is mainly due to the government policy for increasing the subsidy of certain castes and classes, rather than the increa se in target. Consequently, the share of credit in total assistance has declined. The per capita assistance has increased by 83.22 per cent from 1991-92 to 1995-96, but this increase is lower than the increase in total assistance (165.68%) during the same period.

The allocation of financial resources under IRDP has not been fully utilised in the State (Table 4.4). This shows the inability of the government to utilise the available funds for the purpose for which it was meant. Due to the non-utilisation of resources, financial allocation to different blocks as well as the target of beneficiaries has not increased according to the incidence of poverty. This cannot be an exception in the case of Begunia Block.

Selection of Beneficiaries: The selection of beneficiaries in the block is not found to be proper. Table 4.5 shows that about 18.89 per cent beneficiaries were above the poverty line at the time of selection. Further-more the percentage of beneficiaries above the cut off point of Rs.8500/- were 28.89 per cent. This does not satisfy the criteria of selection on the basis of income. Besides the improper selection on the basis of income, the selection is also not faultless on the basis of land holdings. As can be seen from Table 4.6 that about 2.22 per cent of the beneficiaries were large farmers having more than 5 acres of land at the time of selection. Though it is a very small percentage, still it raises doubt about the integrity of the selection procedure.

The above improper selection of beneficiaries is due to the absence of a full scale statistical survey of income and assets and ranking of households with reference to a composite index of land holding and income. Further more, there was no role of Gram Sabha (or village meeting) in selecting beneficiaries. The selection was mostly made by the B.D.O. with the help of a list prepared by the VLW on the basis of income.

The distribution of sample beneficiaries on the basis of their caste and land holding is presented in Table 4.6, where it is found that the SC & ST beneficiaries fall short of the stipulated target of 50 per cent.

Financial Aspects: Table 4.7 presents a picture of average cost of the schemes and its composition. With an average cost of Rs. 6489.32 per beneficiaries, about 60 per cent comes from bank as loan and about 34 per cent as subsidy from the Government. The rest 6 per cent has come from own fund. Hence, the assistance per beneficiary is about 94 per cent, which accounts to an average of about Rs.

6000. The per capita assistance received by the sample beneficiaries (i.e. Rs. 6000) is lower than the figure shown by the block authorities.

On an average 13 mandays had to be spent by the beneficiaries to get the assistance. The beneficiaries had to spend an average amount of Rs. 244 for spending the mandays to visit different offices (Table 4.8a). This is mostly due to the fact that the gap of assistance between the date of submission of application and receipt was too large (Table 4.8b). Besides the mandays spent by the beneficiaries, they had to give an average amount of Rs. 136 as bribe. This shows that the element of bribe is still continuing even though it has been done away with to a great extent in other spheres.

It can be observed from Table 4.9 that about 71.11 per cent of the total sample beneficiaries have loan outstanding of an average amount of Rs.4012.58. Besides this, 55 per cent of them have loan overdues. The most important reason for loan overdues is that about 60 per cent of them have not been invested on the scheme but diverted from other purposes. This diverted fund has been mostly used for consumption purposes. Both the development officials and beneficiaries are responsible for the improper use of funds. While the machinery involved for the implementation has the single minded objective of fulfilling the target at any cost, its role was restricted to disbursement of credit and subsidy only. The officials have not taken any follow-up action so as to avoid such misutilisation. This is becasue it is primarily treated as a soft option by officials to provide the poor with some kind of temporary relief through a subsidised asset. It is also a good option on the part of the beneficiaries to be releived temporarily from their burden either by repaying the earlier loan or by using the money sanctioned for consumption purpose.

Impact of the Programme: Since the objective of IRDP is to generate additional income by creating self-employment, its impact on generating additional income and employment are analysed below:

(a) Income Generation: The impact of IRDP for generating additional income is explained through the reduction in the extent and intensity of poverty.

The average income of the IRDP beneficiaries has increased from Rs. 7752.21 before assistance of Rs. 9036.11 after assistance i.e. by about 17 per cent, indicating that it has not crossed the poverty line of Rs. 11,000/-. Considering the total sample beneficiaries, only 6.67 per cent of them have crossed the poverty line (Table 4.10). This shows that the extent of poverty has been reduced at a very lower rate. This is also observed in different caste groups (Table 4.10). But the performance of beneficiaries crossing the poverty line is found to be better in the higher caste groups as compared to the volnerable sections like SC and ST. While none of the beneficiaries in the ST group has crossed the poverty line, only about 3 per cent of SC group have crossed the poverty line.

Even though a very small percentage of beneficiaries have crossed the poverty line it does not indicate that others have not benefited from the programme. There are some beneficiaries (30 per cent) whose incomes have increased but which are not sufficient to cross the poverty line of Rs. 11,000/- (Table 4.11). The beneficiaries crossing the income level of Rs. 3500/-, Rs. 6400/- and Rs.8500/- are 7.77 per cent, 10.0 per cent and 13.33 per cent respectively (Table 4.11). This shows that intensity of poverty has been reduced, though not to a great extent. The reduction in the intensity of poverty can also be observed from Table 4.12. Here the modal class after assistance remained at the same level as it was before assistance i.e. Rs.3501/- to Rs.6400/-, but with a lower frequency. There is also general movement of the beneficiaries to the higher income class after assistance.

The case-wise and land holding wise reduction in the intensity of poverty among the beneficiaries can be observed from Table 4.13 and Table 4.14 respectively. Here, the model class in different caste groups and land holding groups have remained same with lower frequency or have moved vertically upward. Further-more there is general movement of beneficiaries to the higher income classes. This is also supported by the increase in average income of different caste groups (Table 4.15) and different land holding groups (Table 4.16), except the large farmer. The decline in the coefficient of variation after assistance, as can be seen from Table 4.15 and 4.16, indicates that the intensity of poverty has been reduced for the poorest of poor.

(b) Employment Generation: Since the objective of IRDP is to generate additional income through self-employment, the impact of IRDP on employment generation is discussed here. It can be seen from Table 4.17 that the number of beneficiaries whose total family employment was upto 200 mandays before assistance has declined after assistance. In contrast to this, the number of beneficiaries whose family employment was above 200 mandays before assistance has increased after assistance. This suggests that the programme has contributed to the generation of additional employment. The modal class which was upto 200 mandays before assistance has shifted upward to 201-320 mandays after assistance. The movement of beneficiaries from the lowest employment class before assistance to higher class after assistance is considered as a positive measure of additional employment generation.

Table 4.18 shows that the share of total beneficiaries in the lowest employment group (i.e. upto 200 mandays) has declined from 57.78 per cent before assistance to 31.11 per cent after assistance. On the other hand, there has been as increase in the share of beneficiaries in the employment class 201-320 mandays (by about 7.7 per cent) and above 320 mandays (by about 18.89 per cent) after assistance. The reduction in the percentage share of beneficiaries in the lowest employment class (upto 200 mandays) and increase in the share of beneficiaries in the highest employment class (above 320 mandays) after assistance as compared to before assistance highlight the extent of reduction in unemployment.

The reduction of beneficiaries in the lowest employment class and increase in the highest employment class are also observed in different caste groups, except in the case of ST group of beneficiaries (Table 4.18). In the ST group, the decline in mandays is observed in the lowest as well as highest group. But cooncentration of beneficiaries after assistance is found to be more in the middle employment group (i.e. 201-320 mandays).

Table 4.19 shows that percentage share of beneficiaries in the groups of landless labour and Marginal Farmer has declined after assistance in the employment class upto 200 mandays. In contrast to this, the share of beneficiaries has increased in the employment class to 201-320 mandays and above 320 mandays. Between the Marginal Farmer and Landless Labourer, the share of beneficiaries going to higher employment class after assistance is more in the former as compared to the latter. While in the case of small farmer the share of beneficiaries has increased in the highest class, no change is observed in the other farmer (medium and large) groups.

The increase in the average mandays employment after assistance in all the caste groups shows that the intensity of unemployment has declined. But the decline in the intensity of unemployment is observed to be more in the upper employment class in the case of ST and other caste (General Caste) groups. This is due to the increase in the co-efficient of variation after assistance (Table 4.20). This indicates that the inequality in the distribution of mandays has increased after assistance among the ST and other (General) caste group of beneficiaries. Like the different caste groups, the increase in average employment is observed in all the land holding groups. But the inequality is found to have increased in the case of landless and small farmer groups. On the other hand, the decline in the inequality is observed in the other farmer groups (Table 4.21).

2. Training of Rural Youth and Self-Employment (TRYSEM)

TRYSEM is a supporting component of the IRDP. Started as a centrally sponsored scheme on 15th August 1979, it aims at providing technical and entrepreneurial skill to rural youths from families below the poverty line to enable them to take up income generating activities. This programme has been implemented in the Begunia block since 1981-82.

Targets and Achievements: The targets and achievements of training in Begunia and Orissa are presented in Table 4.22. It can be observed from the table that while the target of training has not been achieved in the state, it has been achieved in the block. It is strange to observe that the target of the number of beneficiaries trained is very small and has been declining since 1992-93. Even in 1994-95, no training was held in the block. Besides the targets of beneficiaries trained, the amount of money sanctioned per capita in the block has declined in the year 1993-94 (Table 4.23). In the year 1994-95, no money was spent for TRYSEM training. Although in 1995-96 the amount utilised for training increased, yet looking at the overall situation, this seems to be not adequate. In the State the amount allocated has not been utilised fully. It is also surprising to note that the percentage of utilisation has been declining over the years. The utilisation has declined from 70.73 per cent in 1991-92 to 33.58 per cent in 1994-95 (Table .23). All these shows that TRYSEM is not given importance at all in the state as well as in the block, though it has great importance.

Selection of Beneficiaries: Like IRDP, the selection of beneficiaries under TRYSEM is not found to be proper. Out of the total sample of 12 beneficiaries 16.67 per cent had the income above the poverty line of Rs.11,000/- while 33.34 per cent had income above the cut off point Rs. 8500/- at the time of selection (Table 4.24).

The share of SC and ST beneficiaries under this programme in the sample is found to be 25 per cent while that of women beneficiaries is 33.33 per cent. This falls short of stipulated target of 50 per cent in the case of SC/ST beneficiaries and 40 per cent in the case of women beneficiaries. Hence, both the identification of beneficiaries and their coverage is not found to be proper.

Impact on Income Generation: About 33.33 per cent of the beneficiaries have crossed the poverty line after assistance. But this cannot be attributed solely to the training programme. As can be seen from Table 4.24 that out of 12 trained beneficiaries only 25 per cent (3 Nos) have taken up the income generating activities on the line of their training. But it is interesting to observe that the percentage increase in mean income is same for those who have utilised the training properly and those who have not utilised at all. Furthermore, the beneficiaries who had lower average income at the time of selection have utilised the training properly. The increase in average income of the beneficiaries who have utilised it indicates that the intensity of poverty has been reduced. The average income of the beneficiaries after assistance is more than the poverty line, which is solely due to the income of the beneficiaries who have not utilised the training (Table 4.24).

From the above it can be inferred that TRYSEM is not a successful programme. This is mostly because it has been treated as a temporary employment programme for getting a stipend.The training is not followed by supply of toolkits, which is essential for the success of TRYSEM. Even though the programme provides some skills to the poor beneficiaries to be self-employed, it cannot be successful one unless the beneficiaries are provided with capital. That is why, it is stipulated that TRYSEM beneficiaries should be given priority for the IRDP scheme, but it is not followed in practice.

Impact on Employment Generation: It can be observed from Table 4.25 that the number of beneficiaries in the employment class upto 200 mandays and 201-320 mandays have declined after assistance. In contrast to this, the number of beneficiaries in the employment class above 320 mandays has increased after assistance. This shows that the intensity of unemployment has declined after assistance. The general movement of beneficiaries from lower employment class before assistance to higher employment class after assistance can be considered as the positive measure of additional employment generation.

The positive measure of additional employment generation can also be seen from different angles. It can be seen from Table 4.25 that the average employment of the beneficiaries who have utilised the training programme properly has increased significantly after assistance as compared to those we have not utilised it at all.

We have earlier observed that the percentage increase is income in both the running and defunct cases is almost same after assistance. But the increase in employment generation at a higher rate in the running cases as compared to defunct cases indicates that, employment generation in the running cases is not effective so as to increase income. This is due to the fact that the training provided in the TRYSEM programme is not sufficient to provide skill and hence is not effective in some cases. The beneficiaries, therefore, have to take full time training (after the TRYSEM training) in private centres with little or no income.

3. Development of Women and Children in Rural Areas (DWCRA)

DWCRA is a sub-scheme of the IRDP. It was started in the year 1982-83 on a pilot basis in 50 districts but has now been extended to all districts of the country. The basic objective of the programme is to provide income generating skills and activities to poor women in rural areas, thereby improving their social and economic status. Through such social and economic empowerment, the programme seeks to improve the access of rural women to health, education, child care, safe drinking water, sanitation, nutrition etc. thereby bringing about an improvement in the quality of life and general well being of the women and children. The women members of DWCRA are required to form groups of 10-15 women for taking up economic activities suited to their skill, aptitude and local conditions. A revolving fund is given to each group to meet its working capital requirements. DWCRA programme has been implemented in Begunia Block since 1994-95.

Targets and Achievements: Table 4.26 presents the target and achievement of beneficiaries in both the block and the state. While the achievement of physical target is very poor at the state level, in the block the target is fully achieved. In Orissa, the percentage of achievement increased from 61.74 per cent in 1994-95 to 89.92 cent in 1995-96, whereas in the block there was cent per cent achievement.

Financial performance of DWCRA in both the block and the state is presented in Table 4.27. It can be observed from the table that amount sanctioned to the block has been utilised fully. But the amount per beneficiary in the block has increased from Rs.1013.33 in 1994-95 to Rs.1258.33 in 1995-96. However, the amount sanctioned per group is not consistent with the stipulated revolving fund. Though in 1994-95, the amount was more than the stipulated amount of Rs.15,000/- per group, in 1995-96 the amount was less than the stipulated amount of Rs. 25,000/-. This is also observed to be true in the state. However, unlike the block, the funds allocated has not been utilised fully in the state. But the percentage of utilisation has increased in 1995-96 from 1994-95.

Selection of Beneficiary: The selection of beneficiaries under DWCRA is not found to be proper. Out of the total sample of 14 beneficiaries only 6 beneficiaries, i.e. 42.96 per cent beneficiaries had the income above poverty line at the time of selection (Table 4.28). On the other hand, 8 out of 14 beneficiaries, i.e. 57.14 per cent had income less than Rs.11,000 stipulated for crossing the poverty line. This indicates that the programme is not wide spread and covers only a few beneficiaries. However, the coverage of SC/ST beneficiaries is 57.14 per cent which is more than the stipulated target of 50 per cent.

Impact of Income Generation: It is interesting to observe that none of the beneficiaries has crossed the poverty line, indicating that the extent of poverty has not been reduced in the DWCRA family (Table 4.28). However, it can be observed that the intensity of poverty has been reduced in the block. The beneficiaries have moved from lower income class before assistance to higher income class after assistance. Due to the reduction in the intensity of poverty the mean income after assistance has increased to Rs.9252.78 from an amount of Rs.8440.20 which was before assistance (Table 4.28). The reduction in the intensity of poverty is also observed among the beneficiaries of different caste groups and landholding groups which can be observed from Table 5.29 and Table 5.30 respectively. Even though the intensity of poverty has been reduced it is of lower scale.

Impact on Employment Generation: It can be seen from Table 4.31 that there is a decline in the number of beneficiaries after assistance in the employment class upto 200 mandays. At the same time the number of beneficiaries after assistance has increased in the employment group to the extent of 201-320 mandays, and above 320 mandays. The movement of beneficiaries from lower employment class to higher employment class is considered as a measure of additional employment generation. The reduction in the number of beneficiaries in the lowest employment groups highlights the extent to which the programme contributed in reducing the number of beneficiaries in the categories of those having the low employment opportunities.

Due to the reduction in the intensity of unemployment the average employment of the beneficiaries has increased significantly from 286 to 460. This shows that the programme is successful in generating additional employment.

The reduction in the intensity of unemployment can also be observed in different caste groups as well as in different landholding groups. From Table 4.32 we observe that the modal classes in different caste groups have shifted upward after assistance. further more, there is general movement of beneficiaries from the lower employment class before assistance to higher employment class after assistance. Like the different caste groups, the modal classes of different landholding groups have shifted upward with the general movement of beneficiaries from lower employment class to higher employment class (Table 4.33). This suggests that the programme has contributed to the increase in employment in different castes as well as land holding groups of beneficiaries.

From the impact of DWCRA on the generation of income and employment, it is observed that DWCRA has created more mandays employment but this has failed to make a break through on the aspect of generation of income. This might be due to the selection of pletty and scattered economic activities. These activities though help the DWCRA groups to employ more persons yet they fail to generate additional income for the beneficiaries. However, two positive points of DWCRA are found . First, the group philosophy is a better idea as it is difficult for poor and particularly for women to sustain individually. Secondly, the promotion of banking habit through introduction of pas books can be noted as a positive feature. This helps the members in DWCRA group to development their saving habit by bringing them close to organise institutional credit agencies.

4. SC and ST Development Finance Cooperative Corporation (DFCC)

In order to uplift the SC/ST people, the government has implemented an important scheme through the Development Finance Cooperative Corporation (DFCC). The scheme is a subsidiary to IRDP scheme. The basis of selection is same as that of IRDP, except it is meant for the SC/ST people. This programme has been implemented in the Begunia block since 1993-94.

Selection of Beneficiaries: The sample beneficiaries under this programme were the poorest of the poor in the sense that their incomes were less than Rs.11,000/- at the time of their selection. There were four beneficiaries in the scheme whose incomes were less than Rs.11,000/- i.e. below the poverty line. This indicates that the selection is proper. All the beneficiaries are found to be SC/ST.

Impact on Income Generation: As can be observed from Table 4.34, none of the beneficiaries has crossed the poverty line after assistance. That means even after assistance, Their income remained below the poverty line of Rs.11,000/-. However, on closer observation it is noticed that the intensity of poverty has been reduced. It can be seen from Table 5.34 that the number of beneficiaries in thc income class before assistance has moved vertically upward after assistance. The modal class has also shifted upward. Due to the reduction in the intensity poverty the average income of the beneficiaries has increased by about 22 per cent from Rs.6004 before assistance to Rs.7326 after assistance. However, this is not a significant performance in increasing additional income of the beneficiaries. The lower performance might to be due the non-existence of asset in the case of 25 per cent of total sample beneficiaries.

Impact on Employment Generation: The impact of the programme on the generation of additional employment is also positive. There is a decline in the number of beneficiaries whose total family employment was upto 200 mandays before assistance. The modal class has shifted upward from the lowest employment class (i.e. upto 200 mandays) before assistance to 201-320 mandays after assistance. Due to the vertical movement of the beneficiaries along the employment class the average mandays employment has increased by 65 per cent (Table 4.25).

5. Fish Farmers Development Agency (FFDA)

FFDA is a subsidiary to IRDP. This programme was started in the Begunia block during 1993-94. The sample covered only one beneficiary under this programme\. It is identified that the selected beneficiary was below the poverty line at the time of selection. He had the real income of Rs.10,714/- which was just below the poverty line of Rs.11,000/- at the time of selection. This shows that the selection was proper.

However, it is surprising to observe that the person has not received any assistance from the Government even though his name was appeared in the official record. It seems that there is leakage somewhere in the system for which the selected person has been excluded from receiving the assistance.

(b) Wage Employment Programmes

1. Jawahar Rojagar Yojana (JRY)

JRY is a centrally sponsored scheme and implemented by the State Governments. It was started in the year 1989-90 with the merger of national Rural Employment Programme (NREP) and Rural Landless Employment Guarantee Programme (RLEGP). It is a rural wage employment programme. The primary objective is to generate addititonal gainful employment for the unemployed and under employed, men and women, in rural areas. The programme aims at providing employment of 100 days to at least one member of each family of rural landless households. Besides the creation of additional employment, it strengthens the rural economic infrastructure. The target group under JRY constitutes people below poverty line, where the preference is given to SC, ST and the freed bonded labourers.

An important feature of JRY scheme is that not only the Panchayats directly receive the money, but the responsibility for executing the programme lies with the village panchayat instead of block officials. This is a positive feature of the scheme.

Targets and Achievements: This programme has been given more importance than the self-employment scheme as the allocation under this programme is significantly more than IRDP in the state. In Orissa, while expenditure under IRDP was Rs.7266.29 lakh in 1995-96, under JRY it was Rs.24683.95 lakh. This is also true in Begunia block. The funds allocated for JRY in the block is significantly more than the subsidy given under IRDP. Even though a significant proportion of fund is allocated to JRY in orissa, the funds utilised are short of the allocation. There is also a declining trend of the percentage of utilisation (Table 4.36). Not only the funds are unutilised fully but also the target of mandays generation is not achieved.

However, in Begunia block the physical target is achieved fully (Table 4.37). The expenditure incurred per mandays generated in Begunia block remains constant over the period from 1991- 92 to 1995-96. This is, however, not so in the State. While the expenditure per manday generated remained more or less constant over the first three years, it increased in 1994-95 and became more than that in Begunia Block.

Impact of the Programme: In the sample of 23 beneficiaries under JRY in Begunia block it is found that they got a total of 896 mandays employment, with an average of 39 mandays per beneficiary. The average wage earned by them is Rs.32/- per day, which is more than the average wage of unskilled labourer declared by the State Government. However, the average employment of 39 mandays is short of the target of creating at least 100 mandays per person. This is not sufficient to lift the poor above the poverty line.

The low mandays of employment created per beneficiary is mostly due to the fact that the fund spread over all the villages is very thin. Besides this, most village panchayats treat JRY mainly as extra income to undertake their activities and not as a programme meant to generate employment and assets for the poor. The primary focus of the programme therefore seems to be on construction of community assets. Assets created were not only of low quality but universally unproductive. School buildings, village community buildings, Harijan houses, roads etc. were some of the items which were built almost everywhere. But the construction of these buildings etc. was of lower quality. On the other hand, the most needed productive assets like repair of ponds, minor irrigation, soil conservation etc. were hardly undertaken anywhere.

(c) Infrastructure Development Programmes

1. Million Wells Scheme (MWS)

The MWS was launched as a sub-scheme of NREP/RLEGP during 1988-89 to provide open irrigation wells, free of cost, to poor small and marginal farmers belonging to SC/ST and freed bonded labourers. From 1989-90, the scheme continued under JRY and since 1996-97 this has become an independent scheme. Since 1993-94, the scheme has been extended to include poor small and marginal farmers belonging to non-SC/ST categories also, subject to the condition that not more than 1/3rd of NWS allocation may be spend on such people.

Targets and Achievements: The physical and financial performance of MWS is presented in Table 4.38. It can be observed from the table that the funds are not fully utilised and the proportion of utilisation is declining since 1992-93. At the same time while the physical target exceeds in three years it falls short in two years. The expenditure incurred per well has been increasing over time. In Begunia block the situation is different. The physical targets have been achieved in all the years and unlike in the state, the expenditure incurred per well has remained unchanged in the last three years (Table 4.39).

Selection of the Beneficiaries: The selection of beneficiaries on the basis of their income is not found to be proper. This is observed from the fact that about 12.90 per cent of the beneficiaries were above the poverty line at the time of their selection (Table 4.40). Further more, 19.35 per cent of the beneficiaries were above the cut-off point of Rs.8,500/-, though they were below the poverty line. However, the random sample shows that less than 1/3rd of the beneficiaries were non-SC/ST, suggesting the proper selection on the basis of caste (Table 4.41). Besides, the selection of beneficiaries on the basis of their landholding is not proper as one beneficiary does not fall on the criteria as the landholding was more than 5 acres (Table 4.42).

Impact on Income Generation: The performance of beneficiaries in terms of reduction in the extent of poverty is not satisfactorily.

Only 6.45 per cent of the beneficiaries have crossed the poverty line after the assistance. On the other hand, the percentage of beneficiaries lying in the lowest income class of upto Rs.3,500/- has increased after assistance.

Table 4.40 shows that the intensity of poverty has declined as the modal class has shifted upward and there is general movement beneficiaries to the higher income class, except in the lowest income class, where the number of beneficiaries has increased after assistance. However, the reduction in the intensity is not found to be satisfactory as it can be observed from Table 4.40 that the increase in the average income is very small.

Table 4.41 and Table 4.42 show the change in the intensity of poverty. The modal class in all the caste groups has shifted upward but at a very lower scale as can by seen from the very small frequency. At the same time it is followed by no general movement of the beneficiaries to the higher income class after assistance.

The lower performance of change in the intensity of poverty in the case of different caste and landholding groups can be seen from Table 4.43 and Table 4.44 respectively. Table 4.43 shows that while the mean income after assistance has declined in the case of SC group of beneficiaries, it has increased in all other caste groups. But the variation is found to be more after assistance, indicating that the intensity of poverty has reduced for the beneficiaries of higher income classes in different groups.

Similar finding is also observed in the case of different landholding groups. Table 4.44 shows that the average income of landless beneficiaries has declined significantly. This indicates that the scheme has not benefited them in generating income. At the same time the increase in the average income along with the coefficient of variation of Marginal Farmer Group shows that the intensity of poverty has declined in the case of higher income group. In the case of small farmers the average income has increased with more or less unchanged coefficient of variation. This indicates that the intensity of poverty has reduced in the case of all groups of Small Farmers.

Impact on Employment Generation: The intensity of unemployment has declined as the number of beneficiaries who had family employment upto 200 mandays (i.e. lowest employment class) has declined from 17 before assistant to 6 after assistance. At the same, the number of beneficiaries having mandays employment of above 320 mandays (i.e. highest employment class has increased from 4 before assistance to 11 after assistance (Table 4.45).

In the different caste groups also the intensity of unemployment has declined. The number of beneficiaries in the lowest employment class has declined after assistance in all the caste groups, except ST group. While in SC group it has declined from 4 to 2, in OBC group it declined from 3 to 1. But in the case of ST group it has increased from 1 to 3. However, in the highest employment class the number of beneficiaries after assistance has increased in all the different caste groups. It has increased from 4 to 7 in case of SC, and from 0 to 2 in case of both ST and OBC (Table 4.45). Due to the decline in the intensity of unemployment the average employment has increased in different caste groups (Table 4.46) with the highest increase in OBC group (37.5 per cent) and lowest in the SC group (18.99 per cent).

The intensity of unemployment has also declined in the case of different land holding groups. In the case of landless labour, while the number of beneficiaries in the lowest employment class has declined from 4 to 3, it has increased in the highest employment class 0 to 1. Similarly, in the case of MF and SF, the beneficiaries in the lowest employment class has declined from 11 to 3 and 2 to 0 respectively. On the other hand, in the highest employment class the number of beneficiaries and increased from 2 to 8 in the case of MF, though it has remained unchanged in the case of SF (Table 4.47). The average employment is different land holding groups has increased due to be reduction in the intensity of unemployment. As can be observed from Table 5.48 that thye increase in mandays employment is highest in the case of MF (30.10 per cent) and lowest in the case of landless group of beneficiaries (23.40 per cnet). The table also shows that the intensity of employment has declined in the highest employment group in the case of landless labourer and lowest employment group in the case of MF and SF.

2. Indira Awaas Yojana (IAY)

Housing is the minimum need for human survival. It is also essential for socio-economic developement. To meet the housing needs of the rural poor, the government has started a programme called 'Indira Awaas Yojana' in May 1985. Initially it was an important component of RLEGP and then remained under JRY from 1989-90. This programme is now being implemented as an independent scheme.

This programme aims at construction of dwelling units free of cost for the poorest of the poor. Freed Bonded labourers, Scheduled Castes and Scheduled Tribes in rural areas are given preference. Some basic features of the scheme are: (a) the order of priority is freed bonded labourers, SC/ST households who are affected by atrocity, floods and other natural calamities and live below poverty line. Households living below poverty line and headed by widows and unmarried women also received priority under the scheme. (b) The allotment of house should be in the name of the female member of the beneficiary household. It may also be in the joint name of both husband and wife: (c) the beneficiaries are to make their own arrangement for construction to suit their requirement; and (d) as far as possible, houses are to be built in cluster so as to facilitate provision of common facilities.

Targets and Achievements: The physical and financial performance of IAY in Orissa is presented in Table 4.49. It has been observed from the table that the funds for IAY in Orissa utilised in excess by about 4.36 per cent, 24.68 per cent and 0.23 per cent than their allocation in 1991-92,1992-93 and 1993-94 respectively. But in 1994-95,the utilisation was about 96.57 per cent of the target. On the other hand, the beneficiaries covered in 1991-92 and 1992-93 were 40.61 per cent and 27.19 per cent more than their targets. However, since 1993-94 the targets have not been fully achieved. The percentages of beneficiaries covered in 1993-94, 1994-95 and 1995-96 are 78.96, 87.40 and 81.06 respectively of the targets. Besides the fluctuations in both the physical and financial targets in Orissa, the cost of construction per house has been increasing. This is in contrast to the expenditure per house in the block.

While expenditure per house in the block has remained constant at Rs.12.70 thousand from 1991-92 to 1993-94, it increased to Rs. 14 thousand in 1994-95 and remained at that level in 1995-96 (Table 4.50, On the othet hand, the targets of covering beneficiaries under IAY scheme have been achieved in the block in all the years, which is in contrast to the state as a whole.

Performance of the Programme: The sample beneficiaries selected under the IAY programme in the block had the income below the poverty line at the time of selection. The beneficiaries are also Scheduled Caste and Scheduled Tribe people. This shows that the selection is proper in the case of beneficiaries under the IAY. The structure of the house of the sample beneficiaries is found to be well designed and constructed. It is noticed in some of the sample selected villages that the houses constructed under IAY scheme were either brick built or stone built. The houses were fairly big to accommodate a large family. It was so constructed that it remained protected from fire and other natural disaster. However, in some other villages the construction of the houses was much below the desired expectations. This might be due to the fact that the houses were built by the constrictors, eventhough it was expected to be built by the beneficiaries.

(B) SOCIAL SECURITY PROGRAMMES

1 Old Age Pension (OAP/WP)

The idea of 'Social Security' is that of using social means to prevent deprivation and vulnerability. Social means can be of various types. Perhaps the most immediate type of social means is to provide direct support to the ability of the vulnerable to acquire the means to basic capacity. Keeping this in view, a number of such schemes have been implemented. Old Age Pension/Widow Pension is one of them. It aims at providing social assistance to the destitutes, who have little or no regular means of subsistence from their own sources of income or through financial support from family members and other sources.

Targets and Achievements: The number of beneficiaries targeted to be covered under OAP/WP scheme was 815 in 1991-92 in the Begunia block and has remained unchanged till 1993-94. This has, however, increased to 2360 in 1994-95 and remained at the level in 1995-96. These targets have been achieved in the different years. The assistance per beneficiary per month has increased from Rs.60/- to Rs.100/- in 1993-94 and remained unchanged till 1995-96 (Table 4.51). But the assistance of Rs.100/- per month is not sufficient to maintain their livelihood. It cannot provide necessary food to the destitutes to make them healthy and active.

Selection of Beneficiary: The selection of beneficiaries under this programme is based on persons who are destitutes with age 65 or more and have no means of livelihood. Besides this, physical and mentally disabled persons and widow are eligible for pensions. Out of the total 22 sample beneficiaries none of them was above poverty line at the time of their selection. But the destitutes upto income Rs. 4000 constitute about 86 per cent of total sample beneficiaries (Table 4.52). This indicates that the selection of the beneficiaries is not confined only to be destitutes. This may be due to the lack of proper survey conducted for selecting the beneficiaries. It was observed during the field study that the list of OAP/WP beneficiaries was prepared by the Sarapanches of the respective areas which the BDO had to oblige. This procedure of selection has its own demerits and is likely to be biased and faulty. That is why many of those eligible do not get benefits.

Impact of the Programme: Even though the main purpose of the programme is to make relief from the destitution, an amount of Rs.100 per month per beneficiary is not sufficient to achieve it. It is like providing dole to the destitutes, for which the quality of life has not uplifted. Besides this, the pension received by the beneficiaries is irregular. Hence, the programme in its present structure is unable to fulfil its objective. There is a need to review the working of this scheme and to design a comprehensive scheme of social security.

The distribution of old age pension is highly uneven. The benefit of the scheme had gone more in favour of those households who had certain connections with local authorities and village headmen. During the course of the survey it was noticed that quite a large number of disabled persons, poor widows, blind persons and helpless inhabitants totally remained outside the purview of the scheme.

Inspite of their representations and repeated requests, the Sarapanch and the block authorities had not taken steps to identify them for receiving the benefit under the scheme.

(c) Food Security Programmes

1. Public Distribution System (PDS)

Public Distribution System as an effective instrument to provide food security is felt by both Politicians and Economists. Since the main cause of hunger is the lack of food security, hunger can be effectively eradicated by PDS. But the effectiveness of the PDS to reduce hunger depends on a number of factors, viz., availability of essential commodities on a regular basis, affordable to the poor in terms of the prices of these commodities vis-a-vis open market, the share of these items in total purchase and the physical access to the fair price shops. The working of PDS in Begunia in the light of above is discussed below.

Availability of Essential Commodities: All the essential commodities supplied through PDS in the State/District are not supplied in Begunia block. The commodities which are not supplied in the block are cloth and palm oil. The share of different commodities supplied through PDS in Begunia is also lower than that in the district (Table 4.53). While the share of rice is marginally lower in Begunia as compared to the district, the shares of other commodities are significantly lower. Considering the supply of rice, the main food of the rural poor, its supply is too low as compared to their demand. Whatever quantity was supplied in 1992-93 if it would have been distributed only among the families below the poverty line, then per household share would not have been more than 10 kg per annum. Hence, it raised the question on the efficacy of PDS to provide food security to the targeted poor in the block. However, in the last year only the supply of rice was significant more, i.e. 60 kg per family per month during 1996-97. But this is a relief measure to get rid of drought and is not likely to be followed in the years to come. Hence, relief measures cannot be a solution to ever-increasing suffering from hunger and poverty.

Access to Food :Even though sufficient rice is given in a drought year about 93.5 per cent of the sample beneficiaries and 97.5 per cent of sample non-beneficiaries have not lifted the full quota (Table 4.54). The reasons for not lifting the full quota is mostly due to the lack of purchasing power on the part of sample beneficiaries and non-beneficiaries. About 62.0 per cent of sample beneficiaries who have not taken the full quota lack of purchasing power. The share is more in the case of non-beneficiaries. For purchasing commodities from PDS the poor require cash payment. But in case of open shops cash payment is not always required, the commodities are also available on credit. Further more, the price of the main food crop i.e. rice, does not differ much between the fair price shop and the open shop.

Physical Access to Fair Price Shop: The poor have also no physical access to the fair price shops. This is due to the lack of time and in some cases distance of the shop from their house. Since most of them are wage earners they have no alternative to forgo their income in order to go to the fair price shop to avail the goods.

Due to the lack of access to food and the fair price shops less than 40 per cent of the total rice expenditure of the sample households come from the fair price shops (Table 5.55) even in a drought year.

From the above observations, it can be inferred that though PDS is an effective instrument to provide food security, it cannot eradicate hunger in the present structure. Hence, this necessitates the need to revamp the PDS.

Apart from rice, kerosene and sugar are other consumable items which are sold through the public distribution system. It is noticed from the field study that in almost all the Panchayats there is greater demand for kerosene oil by beneficiary households but the supply of kerosene was much low to match with growing demand. On an average each beneficiary household receives less than 2 litres of kerosene per month which is grossly inadequate to meet his requirement. Sometimes the unscrupulous activities of dealers also prevent beneficiaries to receive their due share of kerosene quota. The only distribution of sugar. Not only the quantity supplied was low but the high price of controlled sugar too prevents the beneficiary house holds to purchase sugar.

PART II

CRITICAL GAPS AND MISSING LINKS

In the last section, an attempt has been made to discuss how different programmes are operating and their impact on the alleviation of poverty and hunger in the Begunia Block. It has been found that the programme have failed to meet their primary objective of alleviating poverty and hunger. This is also reflected on the increase in the extent of poverty in the block within a period of five years from 1992 to 1997. According to the survey of the block, the number of families below poverty line has increased from 15,803 to 18,488 during the same period. The increase in the number of families below poverty line, despite the implementation of various poverty alleviation programmes indicates that the benefit is not reached to the poor properly. This has the every danger of leading to deprivation and hunger to a large number of families in the block.

The dismal performances of the poverty alleviation programmes are due to a number of critical gaps and missing links. These are found both in the implementation of the programmes as well as in the strategy of different programmes. An attempt has been made here to discuss the problems as found in these two levels. The discussion has been made regarding the general and specific problems encountered in different poverty alleviation programmes in the block.

A. General Problems

1. Problems in the Implementation

A number of critical gaps and missing links are observed in the implementation of different programmes in the block. The most common elements of them are discussed in the following:

(i) Identification of Beneficiaries: The most important leakage in the implementation of different programmes is the defective identification of beneficiaries. Due to the improper identification of beneficiaries, a number of poor families are excluded and the non-poor are included in the beneficiary list. The faulty selections of beneficiaries are due to the following reasons:

(a) Lack of proper norms for estimating income from various activities and lack of vigorous scrutiny by block authorities of the estimates of income prepared by the views.

(b) There is no role of Gram Sabha (Village Meeting) in the selection of beneficaries.

(c) The list of identified target groups as well as selected beneficiaries are not displayed in the public places.

(d) Last, but not the least, the role played by the local politicians and the elite classes are also responsible for the faulty selection of beneficiaries.

(ii) Delay in Loan Disbursement: There is delay in the disbursement of loan in the self-employment programmes, like IRDP. It has been observed that more that 66 per cent of the IRDP beneficiaries received loan after six months of their application (Table 4.8 (b).Due to the delay, the beneficiaries had to lose many working days and to spend money to get the load (Table 4.8 (a).

(iii) Inefficiency and Corruption:There is inefficiency a corruption at all levels. It is difficult to concretise cases of corruption noticed in certain cases. However, there are signs of inefficiency visible in the implementation of serious poverty alleviation programmes in the block. Some instances can be mentioned here:

(a) It has been observed that in Managovindapur village some affluent families got the schemes under IRDP, who had close link with the Block officials.

(b) In some cases bribes are given to officials at the block level for getting the scheme (Table 4.8 (a).

(c) In the selection of beneficiaries under Old Age Pension Scheme the B.D.O. acknowledged the list prepared by the Sanapanches, who have the political bias. In some cases the most needy widows and aged persons failed to get the pensions inspite of several requests.

(d) While installing the million wells, no proper groundwater survey is made, which has resulted in inadequate water in many cases. Besides, in some cases the wells remained dry due to faulty location of wells and for this the villagers suffered a lot.

(e) In some cases loans are not provided to the beneficiaries in actual sense. In such cases, though loan amounts are deposited in the bank on the accounts of the beneficiaries, yet the beneficiaries are not allowed to draw money for installation of the assets. Money so deposited on the bank are adjusted against the load sanctioned to beneficiaries in the shape of book entry..

Due to these inefficiencies, implementation of different programmes became more difficult.

(iv) Lack of Awareness: It has been observed that there is lack of awareness among the poor relating to the objectives, terms and conditions of various programmes. For instance, awareness level of DWCRA is quite low. Most of the members do not know what DWCRA means, what is the status of revolving fund (whether it is a loan or subsidy) etc. In fact, even the staff are not aware of the full scope and aims of DWCRA. That is why the revolving fund account book is kept at the Block office and is operated by the B.D.O. even though the provision is that it is to be operated by the group organiser.

In most of the programmes, extension services are not provided at all so as to make the poor fully aware of the programmes. Due to the lack of awareness, the participation of the poor in different programmes is not encouraged. The extension staff attached to block office failed to motivate the beneficiaries about the positive aspects of the various programmes.

(v) Lack of Follow-up Action: Lack of follow-up action is one of the most important defects observed in the field. There is single minded objective of fulfilling the target at any cost. However, the crucial role of post-disbursement activities like after care support and monitoring is ignored in practice by the development officials.

This has been reflected in the poor status of the assets in different programmes, and more particularly in IRDP. In IRDP, about 70 per cent of the beneficiaries had at the time of survey. Within a period of five years, the assets are found to be damaged or sold out, and in some cases the beneficiaries have not invested on the assets at all. If after care support and monitoring would have been made, such a miserable state of affairs would not have occurred.

Similar is the case in TRYSEM. About 75 per cent of the beneficiaries have not taken up the income generating activities on the line of their training. While the training imparted to the poor is of low quality and of small duration, the training is not followed by supply of capital and toolkits. In the case of DWCRA, the beneficiaries are not provided with proper training in respect of procuring raw materials, marketing of products, etc. which should have been made after disbursing the assistance. In the absence of this, only fulfilling the target will not help in achieving the objective.

Very often training is not conducted at the door step of the beneficiaries i.e. Panchayats and Villages. They are often required to undertake training programmes at the block headquarter or concerned departmental venues located in district headquarter i.e., Khurda. This is both time consuming and resource using as the beneficiaries are to cover a long distance to attend the training by spending their own hard earned money. In majority of cases conveyance allowance given to beneficiaries is not readily disbursed and when the amount is sanctioned it reaches the beneficiaries after a long period of time i.e. much after the training programme is over. From the field study, it is again evident that the training course imparted to them is not of very much practical in nature, it is not continuous. Once the training is given that is not again repeated for the same beneficiaries in order to brush up their interest and aptitude.

(vi) Lack of Proper Coordination: There is poor coordination among the multiple agencies involved in different programmes. For example, in DWCRA, the coordination between the health functionaries and Panchayat/Block functionaries is not encouraging.

2. Problems in the Strategy

Besides the problems in the implementation of different programmes, some defects in the strategy of these programmes are observed. This might have acted for the low performance of programmes in alleviating poverty.

(a) Self-Employment Programme

(i) The self-employment programmes like IRDP, TRYSEM, DWCRA, etc., expect too much in term of entrepreneurial capacity from the poorest of the poor, who neither have the capacity nor the credit worthiness to undertake self- empl- .oyment.

(ii) The self-employment programme like IRDP and isolated from the main growth process in terms of resource allocat- ion,technology and sectoral developement.

(iii) Schemes which are household based are not seen to be integrated with the development needs resource base of the area.

(b) Wage Employment Programme

(i) In the wage employment programme primary focus is given to the creation of asset (Productive or Unproductive), rather than wage employment.

(ii) No specific plan has been formulated to cover all the targeted households and to provide them assured employment of at least 100 days employment.

(c) Infrastructure Development Programmes

(i) It is assumed that those who possess cultivable land can cross the poverty line if infrastructure like wells are provided to them. However, this may not be true in the case of beneficiari es possessing uneconomic land holding.

(d) Social Security Programme

(i) The amount of pension provided through the OAP/WP schem

is not sufficient to improve the quality of life.

(e) Food Security Programme

(i) Distribution of goods through PDS is in general nature cover ing both poor and non-poor, and not specially targeted to the poor.

(ii) All the essential commodities required by the poor are not supplied through PDS.

(iii) The prices of commodities under PDS are not accessible to the poor

(iv) The quantities of different commodities supplied are not suf ficient to maintain their livelihood.

B. Specific Problems

Besides the above common problems observed in the strategy and implementation of different programmes, some specific problems observed in particular programmes are presented in the following;

1. *I.R.D.P.*

(i) The selection of schemes through the choice of beneficiaries as per their requisite skills is not always proper, because over crowding of one scheme means under utilisation of the as sets.

(ii) The necessary backward and forward linkages have not been sttrengthened so as to minimise the risks to the households.

(iii) There is poor integration between IRDP and TRYSEM. Though IRDP schemes should be provided to the TRYSEM beneficia ries, in reality it is not happening in many cases.

(iv) There is too much bureaucratisation and centralisation in plann ing and implementation of the programmes by the officials.

(v) Lack of follow-up action has resulted in non-existence of assets in most of the cases. The difficulties in marketing and production have also cropped up.

2. *TRYSEM*

(i) The trades with which skills are to be developed are identified on the basis of ad hoc consideration.

(ii) The skill imparted are of low standards.

(iii) The training does not always help the poor to improve their levels of living as the needs are not identified after system atic review of demand.

(iv) TRYSEM has failed to impart modern skills for employment in the non-farm sector.

(v) The programme is treated as a temporary employment for getting stipend.

3. *DWCRA*

(i) It relies on blanket guidelines rather than on project approach regarding financial needs, training expenditure etc.

(ii) The assumption of 10 to 15 poor village women, most of whom are illiterate, ignorant and tradition bound, can be capa ble of running a successful business within three to five years, it highly unrealistic. It is not a feasible goal unless the groups are backed by really capable agencies.

(iii) The two major support for women, namely, child care and technology for reducing drudgery, which are import ant components of DWCRA, are ignored in practice.

(iv) There is serious drawbacks in training, difficulties in market ing their products and problems of getting adequate credit.

(v) Lack of orientation of project staff, and insufficient link ages are some of the reasons for inactive groups besides the poor follow up and target chasing.

4. J.R.Y

(i) Most of the assets created through this programme are not not only of low quality but also universally unproductive.

(ii) Employment of at least 100 mandays is not provided to all the poor households who are below poverty line.

5. M.W.S

(i) Amount of assistance provided to the beneficiaries is not suff icient to dig the well in ablock, where ground water is at a very high distance from the surface.

(ii) Proper ground water survey has not been made while install ing the million wells. That is why in some cases water is inadequate for cultivation and even become dry during sum mer season.

(iii) There is no cold storage facility for the farmers,due to which the beneficiaries have to sell the products at a lower price in the local markets or to the middlemen.

6. IAY

(i) Although the beneficiaries have to build their houses on their own choice under the IAY scheme, in practice the contract ors are being appointed for constructing such houses. This result in building of sub-standard house in some cases.

All this shows that different anti-poverty programmes which have been launched by the Government of Orissa have not provided adequate benefit to the poor.

Table 4.1

Physical Performance of IRDP

Year	*Begunia*			*Orissa (thousand)*		
	No. of Families targeted	*No. of Families benefited*	*Achievement (%)*	*No. of families targeted*	*No. of families benefited*	*Achievement (%)*
1991-92	291	300	103.09	111.7	132.9	118.98
1992-93	291	291	100.00	93.20	105.1	112.77
1993-94	470	470	100.00	160.0	172.9	108.06
1994-95	482	391	81.12	135.4	151.70	112.04
1995-96	406	435	107.14	108.0	141.60	131.11

Source: Compiled from P.R.Department, Government of Orissa & Begunia Block, Begunia.

Table 4.2

Share of IRDP Beneficiaries Targeted and Subsidy Allocated to Begunia Block in State Total (in %)

Year	*Share of Beneficiarie Targeted*	*Share of Subsidy allocated*
1991-92	0.26	0.18
1992-93	0.31	0.26
1993-94	0.29	0.24
1994-95	0.36	0.35
1995-96	0.38	0.32

Source: Compiled from P.R. Department, Govern ment of Orissa and Begunia Block, Begunia.

Table 4.3

Subsidy and Credit Disbursement Under IRDP in Begunia

Total	*Total (Rs. in lakh)*			*Per capita (in Rs.)*		
	Subsidy	*Credit*	*Total Asistance*	*Subsidy*	*Credit*	*Total Asistance*
1991-92	5.70	15.89	21.59	1900	5297	7197
	(26.40)	(73.60)	(100.00)			
1992-93	5.92	17.21	23.13	2034	5914	7948
	(25.59)	(74.41)	(100.00)			
1993-94	6.51	20.22	26.73	1385	4302	5687
	(24.35)	(75.65)	(100.00)			
1994-95	14.44	27.16	41.60	3693	6946	10639
	(34.71)	(65.29)	(100.00)			
1995-96	18.09	39.27	57.36	4159	9028	13186
	(31.54)	(68.46)	(100.00)			

Note: Figures in the brackets are percentage share of total assistance.
Source: Office of Begunia Block, Begunia.

Table 4.4

Financial Performance of IRDP in Orissa

Year	*Allocation (Rs.in lakh)*	*Utilisation (Rs. in lakh)*	*Achievement (Percentage)*
1991-92	4492.81	3841.62	85.51
1992-93	3874.98	3373.97	87.07
1993-94	7436.36	6263.38	84.23
1994-95	7986.47	6034.80	74.56
1995-96	8595.64	7266.29	84.53

Source: Government of Orissa, P.R. Department, Bhubaneswar.

Table 4.5

Annual Income of the IRDP Beneficiaries at the time of Selection

Income Class (Rs.)	*No.of Beneficiaries*	*Percentage Share*
Upto 3500	13	14.44
3501-6400	31	34.44
6401-8500	20	22.22
8501-11,000	9	10.00
Above 11,000	17	18.89
Total	90	100.00

Source: Compiled from Field Data.

Table 4.6

Selection of IRDP Beneficiaries According to Caste and Occupation

Caste	*Landless labour*		*Marginal Farmer*		*Small Farmer*		*Other Farmers*		*Total*	
	No.	*%*	*No*	*%*	*No.*	*%*	*No.*	*%*	*No.*	*%*
S.C.	14 (45.16)	43.75	17 (33.33)	53.12	1 (16.67)	4.79	--	--	32 (35.56)	100.0
S.T.	5 (16.13)	55.56	4 (7.84)	44.44	--	--	--	--	9 (10.0)	100.0
O.B.C	825.00 (25.81)	22	68.75 (43.14)	2	6.25 (33.33)	--	--	_	32 (35.56)	100.0
Others	4 (12.90)	23.53	8 (15.69)	47.06	3 (50.00)	17.65	2 (100.0)	11.76	17 (18.89)	100.0
All	31 (100.0)	34.44	51 (100.0)	56.67	6 (100.0)	6.67	2 (100.0)	2.22	90 (100.0)	100.0

Note:(i) Figures in the parentheses are percentage share in all caste group.
(ii) SC= Scheduled Caste, ST=Scheduled Tribe, OBC = Other Backward Caste
Source:Compiled from Field Data.

Table 4.7

Cost- Composition of the Scheme under IRDP

1.	Average Cost (Rs)	:	6489.32
2.	No of Beneficiaries	:	90
3.	Composition of the Cost (in %)		
(a)	Loan	:	59.93
(b)	Subsidy	:	33.87
(c)	Other Sources:	:	6.20
(d)	All	:	100.00

Source: Compiled from Field Data.

Table 4.8 (a)

Mandays and Money Spent to get the Loan/ Assitance in IRDP

1.	Average Mandays Spent		:	13
2.	Average Money Spent (Rs.)			
	(a)	For Transport (Rs)	:	244.37
	(b)	For Bribe (Rs.)	:	136.25
	(c)	All	:	380.62

Source : Compiled from Field Data.

Table 4.8 (b)

Gap Between Application and Receipt of Assistance in IRDP

Duration (Month)	*No. of Beneficiaries*	*% Share*
Upto 3	10	11.11
3-6	23	25.56
Above 6	57	63.33
All	90	100.00

Source: Compiled from Field Data.

Table 4.9

Outstanding Loan and overdue of the IRDP Beneficiaries

			Nos.	%share
1.	Loan Outstanding			
	(a)	No. of beneficiaries :	64	
	(b)	Percentage Share :	71.11	
	(v)	Average Loan Ourtanding (Rs.) :	4012.58	
2.	Overdue			
	(a)	No. of Beneficiaries :	35	
	(b)	Percentage share in total outstanding :	54.69	
	(c)	Average overdue :	4130.41	
3.	Reasons for overdue			
	(a) Sold the asset		5	14.29
	(b) Assets Destroyed		4	11.43
	(c) Not invested in the scheme		21	60.00
	(d) Income generation from asset is not sufficient		3	8.57
	(e) Others		2	5.71

Source : Compiled from Field Data.

Table 4.10

Percentage of IRDP Beneficiaries Crossing the Poverty Line of Rs. 11,000/-

Caste	*Percentage of Beneficiaries above the poverty line*		*Percentage of Beneficiaries*
	Before Assistance	*After Assistance*	
S.C.	12.12 (4)	15.15 (5)	3.03 (1)
S.T.	12.50 (1)	12.50 (1)	0.00 (0)
O.B.C	18.75 (6)	31.25 (10)	12.50 (4)
Others	35.29 (6)	41.18 (7)	5.89 (1)
All	18.89 (17)	25.56 (23)	6.67 (6)

Note: Figures in the parentheses are number of beneficiaries.
Source: Compiled from Field Data.

Table 4.11

Percentage of Beneficiaries Crossing Different Income Levels

Income Level (Rs.)	*Percentage of Before Assistance*	*Beneficiaries After Assistance*	*% Crossing the income level*
Above 3500	85.56	93.33	7.77
Above 6400	51.11	61.11	10.00
Above 8500	28.89	42.22	13.33
Above 11,000	18.89	25.56	6.67

Source: Compiled from Field data.

Table 4.12

Distribution of IRDP Beneficiaries on the Basis of their Income and Average Income of the Beneficiaries

Income Class (Rs.)	*No. of Beneficiaries*		*Average Income*	
	Before Assistance	*After Asssist.*	*Before Assistance*	*After Asistance*
Upto 3500	13	6	2388.69	2906.50
3501-6400	31	29	4593.74	4961.96
6401-8500	20	17	7393.25	7338.88
8501-11,000	9	15	9576.33	9535.73
Above 11,000	17	23	17069.88	16700.73
Total	90	90	7752.21	9036.11

Source: Compiled from Field Data.

Table 4.13

Distribution of IRDP Beneficiaries in Different Caste Groups According to their Income

Income Class (Rs.)	*S.C.*		*S.T.*		*OBC*		*General*		*All*	
	Before Assistance	*After Assist.*	*Before Assistance*	*After Assit.*	*Before Assistance*	*After Assist.*	*Before Assistance*	*After Assist.*	*Before Assistance*	*After Assist.*
Upto 3500	4	2	1	0	7	2	1	2	13	6
3601-6400	10	11	4	2	9	8	8	8	31	29
6401-8500	12	7	1	4	5	6	2	0	20	17
8501-11,000	3	8	1	1	5	6	0	0	9	15
Above 11,000	4	5	1	1	6	10	6	7	17	23
Total	33	33	8	8	32	32	17	17	90	90

Source : Compiled from Field Data.

Table 5.14

Distribution of IRDP Beneficiaries in Different Caste Groups According to their Income

Income Class (Rs.)	*S.C.*		*S.T.*		*OBC*		*General*		*All*	
	Before Assistance	*After Assist.*	*Before Assistance*	*After Assist.*	*Before Assistance*	*After Assist.*	*Before Assistance*	*After Assist.*	*Before Assistance*	*After Assist.*
Upto 3500	5	3	6	3	2	0	0	0	13	9
3501-6400	12	14	16	15	2	0	1	0	31	29
6401-8500	10	7	9	10	1	0	0	0	20	17
8501-11,000	3	4	6	10	0	1	0	0	9	15
Above 11,000	1	3	12	11	3	7	1	2	17	23
Total	31	31	49	49	8	8	2	2	90	90

Note: MF=Marginal Farmer, SF=Small Farmer.
Source: Compiled from Field Data.

Table 4.15

Average Income and Coefficient of Variation in Different Caste groups of IRDP Beneficiaries

Caste	*Average Before Assistance*	*Income After Assistance*	*%change*	*Coefficient of Variation(%) Before Asistance*	*After Assistance.*
S.C.	7257.42	7910.06	8.99	62	53
S.T	6436.37	8059.56	25.21	42	36
OBC	7080.90	9391.50	25.21	42	59
Other	10682.58	11030.05	3.25	94	86
All	7768.64	9040.50	16.37	77.59	67.43

Source: Compiled from Field Data.

Table 4.16

Average Income and Coefficient of Variation in Different Land Holding Groups of IRDP Beneficiaries

Land Holding Group	*Average Income (Rs.)*		*%Change*	*Coefficient of Variation (%)*	
	Before Assistance	*After Assist.*		*Before Assistance*	*After Assist.*
Landless	5526.41	6441.67	16.56	47.08	40.81
M.F	7896.25	9334.27	18.21	69.91	60.86
S.F	15324.00	17626.50	15.02	76.60	61.38
Others	16603.15	16073.35	-3.19	20.45	22.67
All	7768.64	9040.50	16.37	77.59	67.43

Source: Compiled from Field Data.

Table 4.17

Distribution of IRDP Beneficiaries According to Their Mandays Employment both Before and After Assistance

Employment Groups (Mandays)	*Number of Beneficiaries*	
	Before Assistance	*After Assistance*
Upto 200	52	28
201-320	28	35
321-440	4	18
Above 440	6	9
All	90	90

Source: Compiled from Field Data.

Table 4.18

Distribution of Mandays Employment of IRDP Beneficiaries according to their Castes both Before and After Assistance

Caste	*% of Beneficiaries upto 200 Mandays*			*% of Beneficiaries Between 201-320 Mandays*			*% of Beneficiaries above 320 Mandays*		
	Before	After	Diff.	Before	After	Diff	Before	After	Diff.
S.C	54.55	27.27	-27.28	30.30	36.36	6.06	15.15	36.36	21.21
S.T	37.50	25.00	-12.50	37.50	62.50	25.00	25.00	12.50	-12.5
OBC	62.50	31.25	-31.25	34.37	40.62	6.25	3.12	28.12	25.0
Others	64.71	41.18	-23.53	23.53	29.62	5.88	11.76	29.41	17.65
All	57.78	31.11	-26.67	31.11	38.88	7.77	11.11	30.00	18.89

Source: Compiled from Field Data

Table 4.19

Distribution of Mandays Employment of IRDP Beneficiaries according to their Castes both Before and After Assistance

Caste	*% of Beneficiaries Upto 200 mandays*			*% of Beneficiaries Between 201-320 mandays*			*% of Beneficiaries above 320 mandays*		
	Before	*After*	*Diff.*	*Before*	*After*	*Diff*	*Before*	*After*	*Diff.*
Landless	54.84	38.71	-16.13	29.03	32.26	3.23	16.13	29.03	12.90
M.F	67.35	28.57	-38.78	28.57	44.90	16.33	4.08	26.53	22.45
S.F	12.50	12.50	0.00	62.50	37.50	-25.0	25.0	50.00	25.00
Others	50.00	50.00	0.00	0.00	0.00	0. 00	50.00	50.00	0.00
All	57.78	31.11	-26.67	31.11	38.89	7.78	11.11	30.00	18.89

Note: B=Before Assistance, A=After Assistance
Source: Compiled from Field Data

Table 4.20

Average Mandays Employment and Coefficient of Variation under IRDP According to their Caste

Caste Group	*Change in Manday Employment (in %)*	*Coeff. of variation (in %)*	
		Before Assist.	*After Assist.*
SC	23.52	48.25	48.39
ST	34.90	42.47	61.16
OBC	29.69	38.55	38.73
Others	30.36	68.52	73.14

Source: Compiled from Field Data.

Table 4.21

Average Mandays Employment and Coeff. of Variation under IRDP According to their landholds.

Landholding	*Change in Mean Mandays Employment (in %)*	*Coeff. of Variation (in%)*	
		Before	*After*
Landless	23.54	59.09	65.95
M.F	34.87	36.92	36.62
S.F	13.02	36.19	59.51
Others	39.64	71.42	61.32

Soruce: Compiled from Field data.

Table 4.22

Physical Performance of TRYSEM

Year	*Begunia*			*Orissa*		
	Target	*Achievement*	*%Achievement*	*Target*	*Achievement*	*%Achievement*
1991-92	50	50	100.0	25120	25194	100.29
1992-93	58	58	100.0	18070	16785	92.89
1993-94	40	40	100.0	21666	15415	71.15
1994-95	--	--	--	19847	15656	78.88
1995-96	35	35	100.0	18840	16589	88.05

Source: Compiled from P.R. Department, Government of Orissa, and Begunia Block, Begunia.

Table 4.23

Financial Performance of TRYSEM

Year	*Begunia*		*Orissa*		
	Amount Sanction (Rs.)	*Amount Per Capita (Rs.)*	*Allocation (Rs. lakh)*	*Utilisation (Rs.lakh)*	*%of Utilisation*
1991-92	85500	1710	445.23	314.90	70.73
1992-93	99180	1710	533.26	342.13	64.16
1993-94	65550	1639	491.13	256.03	52.13
1994-95	--	--	1138.16	382.14	33.58
1995-96	67500	1929	859.54	670.66	78.03

Source: Compiled from P.R. Department, Government of Orissa, and Begunia Block, Begunia.

Table 4.24

Percentage Distribution of Beneficiaries and Mean Income of the Beneficiaries in different Income Class under TRYSEN

Income Class	*Percentage of Beneficiary*			*Mean Income*		
	Before	*After*	*Diff.*	*Before*	*After*	*Diff.*
Upto 3500	25.0 (3)	0.00	-25.0	2673.6	0.00	-100.00
3501-6400	16.67 (2)	16.67 (2)	0.00	4785.5	5865.5	22.57
6401-8500	25.0 (3)	16.67 (2)	-8.33	6976.0	7435.5	6.59
8501-11,000	16.67 (2)	16.67 (2)	0.00	10714.0	9321.0	-13.00
Above 11,000	16.67 (2)	50.00 (6)	33.33	12473.0	15392.3	23.40
Total	100.0 (12)	100.00 (12)	0.00	7074.50	11466.5	62.08
Not Running		75.0 (9)		7575.6	12282.9	62.14
Running		25.0 (3)		5571.0	9017.3	61.86

Note: (a) Figures in the parentheses are number of beneficiaries.
(b) Running means the assets are in working condition at the time of survey. Nor running means assets are not in working condi tion

Source: Compiled from Field Data.

Table 4.25

Distribution of Beneficiaries and their Mean Employment under TRYSEM

Employment Class	*No. of Beneficiaries*		*Mean Employment*		
	Before	*After*	*Before*	*After*	*%change*
Upto 200	7	5	121.4	140.0	15.32
201-320	4	2	279.0	275.0	-1.33
Above 320	1	5	700.0	511.0	-27.0
Total	12	12	222.0	317.0	42.80
Not running	9	9	232.2	311.67	34.23
Running	3	3	191.7	333.30	73.87

Note : See the notes of Table 4.24.
Source: Compiled from Field Data.

Table 4.26

Pysical Performance of DWCRA

Year	Block				% of Achievement	State		
	Target		Achievement			Target	Achievement	
	persons	No. of groups	persons	No. of groups		No. of groups	No. of groups	% achievement
1994-95	60	4	60	4	100.00	1192	736	61.74
1995-96	120	8	120	8	100.00	1924	1730	89.92

Source: Compiled from P.R. Department, Govt. of Orissa, and Begunia Block, Begunia.

Table 4.27

Pysical Performance of DWCRA

Year	Block					State			
	Amount of sanction (Rs.)	*Utilisation (Rs.)*	*% of Utilisation*	*Amount per group (Rs.)*	*Amount per beneficiary (Rs.)*	*Allocation (Rs. lakh)*	*Utilisation (Rs. lakh)*	*% of Uti per group*	*Amount per group (Rs.)*
1994-95	60,800	60,800	100	15,200	1013	140.87	112.43	79.81	15,275
1995-96	1,51,000	1,51,000	100	18,875	1258	388.38	322.72	83.09	18,654

Source: Compiled from P.R. Department, Govt. of Orissa, and Begunia Block, Begunia.

Table 4.28

Distribution of Beneficiaries and their Mean Income in Different Income Class Under DWCRA

Income Class	*No. of Beneficiary*		*Mean Income*	
	Before	*After*	*Before*	*After*
Upto 3500	2 (14.29)	0	1339.0	0
3501-6400	6 (42.86)	4 (28.57)	5364.50	4535.25
6401-8500	0	4 (28.57)	0	0
8501-11,000	0	0	0	0
Above 11,000	6 (42.86)	6 (42.86)	3883.0	13882.16
Total	14 (100.00)	14(100.00)	8440.20	9252.78

Note: Figures in the parentheses are percentage share of the total Source: Compiiled from Field Data.

Table 4.29

Distribution of DWCRA Beneficiaries on the Basis of their Caste and Income

Income Range (Rs.)	*S.C*		*S.T*		*OBC*		*Other*		*ALL*	
	B	*A*	*B*	*A*	*B*	*A*	*B*	*A*	*B*	*A*
Upto 3500	1	0	0	0	0	0	1	0	2	0
3501-6400	3	4	0	0	2	0	1	0	6	4
6401-8500	0	0	0	0	0	2	0	2	0	4
8501-11,000	0	0	0	0	0	0	0	0	0	0
Above 11,000	3	3	1	1	1	1	1	1	6	6
Total	7	7	1	1	3	3	3	3	14	14

Source: Compiled from Field Data.

Table 4.30

Distribution of DWCRA Beneficiaries on the Basis of their Caste and Income

Income Class (Rs.)	*L.L*		*M.F*		*S.F*		*ALL*	
	B	*A*	*B*	*A*	*B*	*A*	*B*	*A*
Upto 3500	1	0	1	0	0	0	2	0
3501-6400	5	4	1	0	0	0	6	4
6401-8500	0	2	0	2	0	0	0	4
8501-11,000	0	0	0	0	0	0	0	0
Above 11,000	1	1	4	4	1	1	6	6
Total	7	7	6	6	1	1	14	14

Source: Compiled from Field Data

Table 4.31

Distribution of DWCRA Beneficiaries and their Mean Employment on the Basis of their Mandays Employment

Employment Mandays	*No. of Beneficiaries*		*Mean Employment*	
	Before	*After*	*Before*	*After*
Upto 200	8 (57.14)	0	176.2	0
201-320	3 (50.0)	7 (50.0)	260.0	298.6
Above 320	3 (50.0)	7 (50.0)	202.0	514.3
Total	14 (100.0)	14 (100.0)	286.40	406.40

Note: Figures in the parentheses are percentage share of total.
Source: Compiled from Field Data.

Table 4.32

Distribution of DWCRA Beneficiaries on the Basis of their Caste and Income

Emploment (Mandays)	*S.C*		*S.T*		*OBC*		*Other*		*TOTAL*	
	B	*A*	*B*	*A*	*B*	*A*	*B*	*A*	*B*	*A*
Upto 200	3	0	1	0	2	0	2	0	8	0
201-320	1	4	0	0	1	1	1	2	3	7
Above 320	3	3	0	1	0	2	0	1	3	7
Total	6	7	1	1	3	3	3	3	14	14

Source: Compiled from Field Data.

Table 4.33

Distribution of DWCRA Beneficiaries on the Basis of their Occupation and Mandays Employment

Employment (Mandays)	*L.L*		*M.F*		*S.F*		*TOTAL*	
	B	*A*	*B*	*A*	*B*	*A*	*B*	*A*
Upto 200	3	0	4	0	1	0	8	0
201-320	3	5	0	2	0	0	3	7
Above 320	1	2	2	4	0	1	3	7
Total	7	7	6	6	1	1	14	14

Source: Compiled from Field Data

Table 4.34

Distribution of DFCC Beneficiaries on the Basis of their Income

Income Class	*Before Assistance*	*After Assistance*
0-3500	0	0
3501-6400	2	0
6401-8500	2	1
8501-11,000	0	3
Above 11,000	0	0
All	4	4

Source : Compiled from Field Data.

Table 4.35

Distribution of DFCC Beneficiaries on the Basis of their Employment

Income Class	*Before Assistance*	*After Assistance*
0-200	4	1
201-320	--	2
Above 320	--	1
All	4	4

Source: Compiled from Field Data.

Table 4.36

Performance of JRY in Orissa

Year	Financial Performance (Rs. in lakh)			Physical Performance (Mandays in lakh)			Exp.per Manday Generated (Rs.)
	Allocation	*Expenditure*	%	*Target*	*Achievement*	%	
1991-92	15422.21	14033.59	72	346.44	348.66	101	40.23
1992-93	14638.02	13067.13	91	340.33	326.39	96	40.04
1993-94	23062.54	19582.43	85	517.14	479.06	93	40.88
1994-95	23330.34	18739.89	80	522.34	443.59	85	42.25
1995-96	32102.34	24683.95	77	599.45	586.04	98	42.12

Source: Compiled from data available in P.R. Department, Government of Orissa.

Table 4.37

Performance of JRY in Begunia

Year	*Physical Performance*		*%*	*Funds allocated (Rs.)*	*Expenditure per Manday generated (Rs.)*
	Mandays Targeted	*Mandays generated*			
1991-92	43607	43607	100	1816980	41.67
1992-93	46488	46488	100	1937022	41.67
1993-94	63257	63257	100	2635725	41.67
1994-95	61629	61629	100	2567684	41.67
1995-96	64964	64964	100	2706870	41.67

Source: Compiled from Field Data availabe in Begunia Block, Begunia.

Table 4.38

Performance of MWS in Orissa

Year	Financial Performance			Physical Performance			Exp. per well (Rs. in thousand)
	Allocation (Rs. in lakh)	Exp. (Rs. in lakh)	%	Target (in No.)	Achievement	%	
1991-92	3168.70	2621.64	83	17460	21394	123	12.25
1992-93	3165.49	3101.41	98	17200	21126	123	14.68
1993-94	5079.40	3427.97	67	34022	21324	63	16.08
1994-95	7418.44	4285.22	58	44413	26113	59	16.41
1995-96	N.A	4322.29	NA	18637	24263	130	17.81

Note: NA = Not Available
Source: Compiled from Field Data.

Table 4.39

Performance of MWS in Begunia

Year	*Physical Performance*		*%*	*Funds All-cated*	*Exp.per well (Rs. thousand)*
	Target	*Achievement*			
1991-92	25	25	100	330000	13.20
1992-93	84	84	100	1254120	14.93
1993-94	137	137	100	2219400	16.20
1994-95	92	92	100	1490400	16.20
1995-96	213	213	100	3450600	16.20

Source: Compiled from Field Data.

Table 4.40

Distribution of Beneficiaries and their Mean Income in Different Income Class under MWS

Income Range	*No. of Beneficiary*		*Mean Income*	
	Before	*After*	*Before*	*After*
Upto 3500	3 (9.68)	5 (16.13)	2401.3	2710.4
3501-6400	9 (29.03)	7 (22.58)	4831.3	5161.1
6401-8500	9 (29.03)	5 (16.13)	7205.8	7350.8
8501-11,000	6 (19.35)	8 (25.81)	9682.3	10104.6
Above 11,000	4 (12.90)	6 (19.35)	20013.0	17382.0
Total	31 (100.0)	31 (100.0)	8270.7	8767.51
Not running	5 (16.13)	5 (16.13)	8300.2	9357.8
Running	26 (83.87)	26 (83.87)	8265.0	8645.0

Note (a) Figures in the parentheses are percentage share of total.
(b) Running means assets in working condition, Not-running means assets not exist at all.

Source: Compiled from Field Data.

Table 4.41

Distribution of MWS Beneficiaries on the basis of their Caste and Income

	S.C		S.T		O.B.C		Others		Total Caste	
	Before	After	Before	After	Before	After	Before	After	Before	After
0-3500	2	3	1	2	0	0	0	0	3	5
3501-6400	4	3	5	2	0	2	0	0	9	7
6401-8500	2	2	3	3	2	0	1	0	8	5
8501-11,000	3	4	1	2	3	2	0	0	7	8
Above 11,0000	2	1	2	3	0	1	0	1	4	6
Total	13	13	12	12	5	5	1	1	31	31
	(41.94)	(41.94)	(38.71)	(38.71)	(16.13)	(16.13)	(3.23)	(3.23)	(100.00)	(100.00)

Note: Figures in the parentheses are percentage share of total caste group.

Source: Compiled from Field Data.

Table 4.42

Distribution of MWS Beneficiaries on the basis of their Land Holding and Inocme

Income Range	*S.C*		*S.T*		*O.B.C*		*Others*		*Total*	
	Before	*After*	*Before*	*After*	*Before*	*After*	*Before*	*After*	*Before*	*After*
0-3500	0	3	3	2	0	0	0	0	3	5
3501-6400	2	1	6	6	1	0	0	0	9	7
6401-8500	3	0	4	4	1	1	1	0	8	5
8501-11,000	0	0	6	8	1	0	0	0	7	8
\Above 11,0000	0	1	3	2	0	2	1	1	4	6
Total	5	5	22	22	3	3	1	1	31	31

Source: Compiled from Field Data.

Table 4.43

Average Income and Coefficient of Variation in Different Caste Groups of MWS Beneficiaries

	Average Income (Rs.)		*% Change*	*Coeffieient of variation (%)*	
	Before Assistance	*After Assistance*		*Before Assistance*	*After Assistance*
S.C.	8895.00	8810.92	-0.94	94.64	95.43
S.T.	7544.91	8267.50	9.57	52.66	53.02
O.B.C	8345.00	9378.00	12.37	15.02	32.42
Others	8491.00	11151.00	31.32	0.00	0.00
Total	8270.74	8767.51	6.01	73.00	138.80

Source: Cofmpiled from Field Data.

Table 4.44

Average Income and Coefficient of Variation in Different Land Holding Groups in MWS Beneficiaries

	Average Income (Rs.)		% Change	*Coeffieient of variation (%)*	
	Before Assistance	*After Assistance*		*Before Assistance*	*After Assistance*
Landless	6459.62	5101.40	-21.03	24.00	64.13
M.F.	7521.68	9208.50	22.43	51.03	82.72
S.F	7634.66	12428.33	62.79	24.84	24.17
Others	35714.00	36214.00	1.40	0.00	0.00
Total	8270.74	8767.51	6.01	73.00	138.80

Source: Cofmpiled from Field Data.

Table 4.45

Distribution of MWS Beneficiaries on the basis of their Caste and Mandays Employment

Manday Employment	*S.C*		*S.T*		*O.B.C*		*Others*		*Total Caste*	
	Before	*After*	*Before*	*After*	*Before*	*After*	*Before*	*After*	*Before*	*After*
Upto 200	4	2	10	3	3	1	0	0	17	6
201-320	5	4	2	7	2	2	1	1	10	14
Above 320	4	7	0	2	0	2	0	0	4	11
Total	13	13	12	12	5	5	1	1	31	31

Source: Compile from Field Data.

Table 4.46

Average Mandays Employment and Coefficient of Variation under MWS According to the Different Caste Groups of Beneficiaries

Caste Groups	*Average Mandays Employment*		*% Change*	*Coeffieient of variation (%)*	
	Before Assistance	*After Assistance*		*Before Assistance*	*After Assistance*
S.C	297.69	354.23	18.99	53.91	45.15
S.T	177.50	237.91	34.03	20.71	26.29
O.B.C	224.00	30/8.00	37.50	21.42	19.08
Others	300.00	360.00	20.00	0.00	0.00
Total	239.35	301.93	26.14	50.76	41.44

Source: Compiled from Field Data

Table 4.47

Distribution of MWS Beneficiaries on the basis of their Land Holdings and Mandays Employment

Manday Employment	*Landless*		*M.F*		*S.F*		*Others*		*Total*	
	Before	*After*	*Before*	*After*	*Before*	*After*	*Before*	*After*	*Before*	*After*
Upto 200	4	3	11	3	2	0	0	0	17	6
201-320	1	1	9	11	0	2	0	0	10	14
Above 320	0	1	2	8	1	1	1	1	4	11
Total	5	5	22	22	3	3	1	1	31	31

Source: Compile from Field Data.

Table 4.48

Average Mandays Employment and Coefficient of Variation under MWS According to the Different land holding Group of Beneficiaries

Land-holding Groups	*Average Mandays Employment*		*% Change*	*Coefficient of variation (%)*	
	Before Assistance	*After Assistance*		*Before Assistance*	*After Assistance*
Landless	188.00	232.00	23.40	31.45	39.63
M.F	220.45	286.81	30.10	31.67	27.54
S.F	300.00	386.66	28.88	47.14	39.91
Others	730.00	730.00	0.00	0.00	0.00
Total	239.35	301.93	26.14	50.76	41.44

Source: Cofmpiled from Field Data.

Table 4.49

Performance of IAY in Orissa

Year	Financial Performance			Physical Performance			Exp per house
	Allocation (Rs. lakh)	Exp. (Rs. lakh)	%	Target (Nos)	Achievement (Nos)	%	(Rs. thousand)
1991-92	2011.89	2099.51	104.36	12110	17028	140.61	12.33
1992-93	1124.78	1402.39	124.68	8888	11305	127.19	12.41
1993-94	1431.50	1434.83	100.23	13410	10588	78.96	13.55
1994-95	2010.91	1942.02	96.57	15214	13297	87.40	14.60
1995-96	N.A	7494.88	N.A	62958	51033	81.06	14.69

Note : NA = Data not available.
Source :Cofmpiled from P.R. Department, Government of orissa.

Table 4.50

Performance of IAY in Begunia

Year	*Physical Target*	*Performance Achieve-ment*	*%*	*Funds Allocated (in Rs.)*	*Exp.per house constructed (Rs in thousand)*
1991-92	10	10	100.0	127000	12.70
1992-93	10	10	100.0	127000	12.70
1993-94	25	25	100.0	317500	12.70
1994-95	48	48	100.0	672000	14.00
1995-96	121	121	100.0	1694000	14.00

Source: Compiled from Block Office, Begunia.

Table 4.51

Performance of OAP Beneficiaries in Begunia

Year	Physical Performance			Amount Sanctioned (Rs.)	
	Target	Achievement	% Achieved	Total	Per beneficiary
1991-92	815	815	100.0	48,900	60
1992-93	815	815	100.0	48,900	60
1993-94	815	815	100.0	81,500	100
1994-95	2360	2360	100.0	2,36,000	100
1995-96	2360	2360	100.0	2,36000	100

Source: Block Office, Begunia.

Table 4.52

Annual Income of the OAP Beneficiaries at the time of Selection

Annual Income (Rs.)	*No. of Beneficiaries*	*% Share*
Upto 4000	19	86.36
4000-6400	1	4.55
6400-8500	1	4.55
8500-11,000	1	4.55
Above-11,000	0	0.00
All	22	100.00

Source : Compiled from Field Data.

Table 4.53

Allotment of Essential Commodities during 1993

Commodities	Begunia	Khurda
Rice (MT)	150 (1.45)	2454 (1.63)
Wheat (MT)	670 (6.49)	31708 (21.11)
Sugar (MT)	348 (3.37)	9962 (6.63)
Kerosene (Kilo Lit)	474 (4.59)	10873 (7.24)
Edible Oil	0	9000 (5.99)

Note: Figures in parentheses indicate allocation per thousand population.
Source: Compiled from the District Statistical Handbook of Khurda, Directo rate of Economics & Statistics, Government of Orissa, 1993.

Table 4.54

Reasons for not taking the Full Quota from PDS

Region	*Beneficiary*					*%notTaking*	*Non-Beneficiary*					*% not Tak-*
	a	b	c	d	Total	Full Quota	a	b	c	d	Total	ing full Quota
Central	7	22	1	4	34	85.00	1	7	0	0	8	100.00
	(20.59)	(64.71)	(2.94)	(11.76)	(100.00)		(12.50)	(87.50)			(100.00)	
North	8	23	6	10	47	94.00	0	9	0	1	10	100.00
	(17.02)	(48.94)	(12.77)	(21.28)	(100.00)		(0.00)	(90.00)		(100.00)	(100.00)	
South	14	71	12	9	106	96.36	1	20	0	0	21	95.45
	(13.21)	(66.98)	(11.32)	(8.49)	(100.00)		(4.76)	(95.24)			(100.00)	
Block	29	116	19	23	187	93.50	2	36	0	1	39	97.50
	(15.51)	(62.03)	(10.16)	(12.30)	(100.00)		(5.13)	(92.31)		(2.56)	(100.00)	

Note a = Not necessary to purchase full guota.
b = Not accessible due to lack of purchasing power
c = Not supplied by the dealer
d = Any other

Source : Compiled from Field Date.

Table 4.55

Household Share of Monthly Rice Expenditure from PDS in the total Cereal Expenditure

Region	Monthly Household Expenditure of rice from PDS (Rs.)		Monthly Household Expenditure of total rice (Rs.)		Percentage share of exp.on rice from PDS to total rice Exp.	
	Beneficiary	Non-Ben.	Beneficiary	Non-Ben.	Beneficiary	Non-Ben.
Central	198.32	20.29	523.06	285.10	37.92	7.12
North	221.00	198.40	507.33	396.33	43.56	50.06
South	158.84	106.38	475.90	320.77	33.36	33.16
Block	192.72	108.36	502.10	334.07	38.38	32.44

Source: Compiled from field data

5

Socio-Economic Conditions of Sample Beneficiary and Non-Beneficiary Households

The main purpose of this chapter is to observe two things: first, how the Government programmes have influenced the socio-economic conditions of sample beneficiaries? Second, how far the socio-economic conditions of beneficiaries are different from the non-beneficiaries. The following sections analyse these points.

Social Composition

The coverage of sample SC and ST beneficiaries is 49.5 per cent of the total sample in the block. This is, however, lower than the share of sample non-beneficiaries (60 per cent). The share of sample SC and ST beneficiaries is found to be consistant with the stipulated share of beneficiaries (50 per cent) to be covered. In spite of this, the inter-regional variation is still found. In the central region the coverage of sample SC & ST beneficiaries is 65.0 per cent, which is more than the stipulated share of 50 per cent. On the other hand, in the north and south regions, the coverages of sample SC & ST beneficiaries are 44.0 per cent and 46.4 per cent respectively, which are less than the stipulated share.

In contrast to the coverage of sample SC & ST beneficiaries, the coverage of sample SC & ST non-beneficiaries is 50 per cent in the north region and more than 50 per cent in both central and month regions (Table 5.1). This indicates that the coverage of sample SC & ST non-beneficiaries is more than sample SC & ST beneficiaries. However, this may not affect the analysis on socio-economic condition much as the variation is not very significant.

Considering the average size of family members, it can be observed from Table 6.1 that the average size of sample beneficiary households is more than 5 in the block as well as in different regions. This is, however, in contrast to the average size of sample non-beneficiary households, which is less than 5 in the block as well as in all the regions.

Agricultural Situation

The condition of sample beneficiaries in the block in respect of their land and water resources is still poor. While about 67.0 per cent of the sample beneficiaries have some amount of land, their land holding size is only 1.56 acres (Table 5.2). Their irrigation condition is not better. Though about 12.92 per cent of their land is irrigated. This is, however, higher than the block average, which is less than 10.0 per cent (Table 5.19). The higher proportion of irrigated area of the sample beneficiaries as compared to the block average is mainly due to the Million Wells Scheme provided to the beneficiaries. But the share of irrigated land constituting 12.92 per cent is not comparable with the state average, which is more than 30 per cent.

In contrast to the sample beneficiaries, the share of cultivators in the non-beneficiaries is only 12.50 per cent with the average land-holding size of 0.48 acre (Table 5.2). Their lands are not irrigated at all.

Another interest thing observed is that above 11 per cent of the beneficiary households, belonging to the category of cultivators, have leased out their land. However, such cases are not observed in the case of non-beneficiaries. On the other hand, the percentage share of leased-in land in the case of non-beneficiary households (57.89 per cent) are observed to the significantly higher than that in the case of beneficiary households (33.20 per cent) (Table 5.2).

Considering inter-regional variation of agricultural situation among the sample beneficiaries and non-beneficiaries, it can be observed from Table 5.2 that the share of cultivating household in the south region is highest. This is followed by the share in central region and north region both in the cases of beneficiary and non-beneficiary households. But the average size of land holding is reverse in the case of beneficiary household i.e. with the highest size in north and lowest in south region. However, this is not so in the case of non-beneficiary households. Their average size of land holding is highest in the south region and lowest in the north region. The percentage share of irrigated land among the sample beneficiaries is highest in the central region (22.92 per cent) and lowest in the north region (2.28 per cent). But there is no irrigated land in the case of non-beneficiaries in any of the regions. It may also be observed from the Table that the leased-out beneficiary households are highest in north region (16.13 per cent) and lowest in South region, but no such leased-out non-beneficiary households are observed in any region. In contrast to this, the leased-in and of non-beneficiary households is observed in central and south regions with the highest share in the case of former than that in the case of latter. But the share among the beneficiary households is highest in such region and lowest in north region. All these show that the south region has done well in respect of agricultural performance and north region has shown a lower performance. The performance of central region lies in between.

Asset Position

It can be observed from Table 5.3 that more than 50 per cent of the sample beneficiaries have assets valued less than Rs. 25,000/-. The situation is more serious in the case of non-beneficiaries. While 97.5 per cent of non-beneficiaries have assets valued less than Rs.25,000/-, with about 55 per cent having asset worth upto Rs.5,000/-.

However, inter-regional variation is observed among both the beneficiaries and non-beneficiaries. While the share of beneficiaries having value of assets less than Rs.25,000/- is highest in north region (56 per cent), it is lowest in central region (50 per cent). On the other hand, there is wide variation in central region in case of non-beneficiaries. While about 75 per cent of them having asset valued upto Rs.5,000/-, about 12.5 per cent have assets valued more than Rs. 25,000/- In north and south regions not much variation is observed among the non-beneficiaries.

Comparing the value of asset of average household, it is observed from Table 5.4 that beneficiary households have a significantly higher value of asset than that of the non-beneficiary households. It is true not only in total but also in different regions. Within different regions the value of assets of average beneficiary household in north is significantly more than the other two regions.

In the case of beneficiary households the share of value of non-productive assets is about 45.0 per cent of which household asset only constitutes about 43.0 per cent and durable assets like cycle, radio, etc. constitute 2.43 per cent (Table 5.4). Among the productive asset the share of agricultural asset (including land holding) is the only major source of income earning of the beneficiaries. Besides this, the value of trees and plants, and bovine population throw some light for their livelihood.

Unlike the beneficiaries, the share of non-productive asset in the case of non-beneficiaries has a significantly higher share then the productive assets. Furthermore, the share of agricultural asset (including land holding) in the case of non-beneficiaries is significantly lower than that in the case of beneficiaries. It can also be observed from Table 5.4 that while the average beneficiary household possesses some non-farm implements (1.12 per cent) and financial assets (1.90 per cent) no such assets are possessed by the non-beneficiary households.

Comparing the share of the value of different assets in different regions., it is observed that though the share of total non-productive asset (household and durable assets) is lower than that of productive asset in the case of beneficiaries in all the regions, the share of non-productive asset in central region is about 49.0 per cent, which is more than both north and south regions (45.0 per cent in each case). In the case of non-beneficiaries the share of non-productive assets in north region is about 95.0 per cent as compared to about 63.0 per cent in central and 72.0 per cent in south region.

Income Pattern

It can be observed from Table 5.5 that income of the beneficiaries from wage has the highest share (32.40 per cent). It is strange that even after getting assistance for self-employment, wage becomes the main source of income in the block as well as in different regions. Next to wage, agricultural becomes the important source of income and constitutes about 22.98 per cent. These two together constitute more than 55.0 per cent of the total income. The other important sources of income are remittances (9.87 per cent) and non-farm sector (7.21 per cent). The significant proportion of income from remittances indicates that due to lack of employment opportunities in the block poor households find their own way of livelihood by migrating outside.

Like the beneficiaries, the income of non-beneficiaries comes mainly from wage, but the share is significantly more than the beneficiaries (Table 5.5). While about 74.36 per cent of income of the beneficiaries comes from wage, the share of income from farm is less than 5.0 per cent which is less than the share of non-farm sector (5.80 per cent). The non-beneficiaries also depend on remittances, whose share is 4.74 per cent in the total income. Besides the above discouraging pattern of income, the average income of non-beneficiary households (Rs. 4797) is less than half of the income of beneficiaries (Rs.11,419). All these show that there is extreme poverty and hunger among the non-beneficiary households.

Inter-regional variation of income of beneficiaries can also be observed from Table 5.5. The income of beneficiaries in north region, from agricultural sector and remittances is higher than the central and south region, while non-farm income is higher in central region and income from activities allied to agriculture is more in south region. Beside this, the wage income in north region is lower than both central and south regions.

Compared between the income of beneficiaries and non-beneficiaries in different regions, it can be observed from Table 6.5 that wage income of non-beneficiaries has a higher share than beneficiaries in all the regions. Besides this, incomes of non-beneficiaries from non-farm sector in north region and from activities allied to agriculture in central region have higher share as compared to the beneficiaries in respective regions.

Pattern of Expenditure

Average expenditure of beneficiary household on food items constitutes about 70.0 per cent of the total expenditure on all commodities (Table 5.6). Within the food items, expenditure on rice has the significant share. Besides the food expenditure, the beneficiary households spend a significant proportion on clothing and health. These two alone constitute nearly 15.0 per cent. The expenditure on these two items together is nearly Rs.2,000/- per annum, of which health expenditure is Rs.673/-. This pattern of expenditure shows that the consumption bundle of the beneficiaries is only for sustainance. However, this consumption bundle is also not met by their income. It can be observed that while the average per capita expenditure of the beneficiaries is Rs.12969.30 (Table 5.6), the average per capita income is Rs.11,418.97 (Table 5.5) only making a shortfall of Rs.1550.33. This shows that even with the assistance the beneficiaries are unable to generate income to meet expenditure.

The case of non-beneficiaries is more serious than the beneficiaries. Though the expenditure of non-beneficiaries is about half of the beneficiaries, it is not met by their income. While average per capita expenditure of the non-beneficiaries is Rs. 6776.28 (Table 5.6), the average per capita income is Rs.4797.40 (Table 5.5) only making a short fall of Rs.1978.88. Therefore, the short fall of income to meet the expenditure in the case of non-beneficiaries is more than the beneficiaries. This is obvious due to the significantly lower income of the former than the latter. In the case of non-beneficiaries the expenditure on food items alone is not met by their income. That means due to low purchasing power the non-beneficiaries have no access to adequate food. This indicates that there is acute hunger among the sample non-beneficiaries in the block.

Considering the inter-regional variation of consumption expenditure, it can be observed from Table 5.6 that the average expenditure of the non-beneficiaries is lower than the average expenditure of the beneficiaries in all the regions. In the case of beneficiaries the average expenditure is highest in the central region (Rs.14,192) and lowest in the north region (Rs. 11,332). But in the case of non-beneficiaries the expenditure is highest in south region (Rs.7583.25) and lowest in central region (Rs.5297.87). Consider the different items of expenditure, it is observed that the south region which has a better health and education facilities command more expenditure than other regions in the case of non-beneficiaries and to extent in the case of beneficiaries. Food item, which commands a highest share of expenditure, remains more or less the same in different regions in the case of beneficiaries. On the other hand, there is a variation in the share of expenditure on food item in different regions in the case of non-beneficiaries. The share remains highest in central and lowest in the south region (Table 5.6).

The per capita consumption of cereals, viz., rice, is less than the recommended cereal intake of 500 gram per day per person in the case of both beneficiaries and non-beneficiaries (Table 5.7). However, the consumption of cereal in the case of non-beneficiaries is more than that of the beneficiaries. This is also observed in different regions, except the south region where the equal amount of cereal is consumed by both beneficiaries and non-beneficiaries. This might be due to the fact that the lower purchasing power of non-beneficiaries compels them to consume more of cereals and less of non-cereal food items than the beneficiaries. Even to consume this amount of cereals the non-beneficiary households have to borrow from their relatives or the money lenders. This shows that hunger is widespread among the non-beneficiaries in the block. Comparing between different regions, per capita consumption of cereals of beneficiary households is highest in the central region and lowest in the north region. On the other hand, per capita consumption of cereals of non-beneficiary households is highest in the north region and lowest in the south region.

Indebtedness

It can be observed from Table 5.8 that about 99.5 per cent of beneficiary households have loan outstanding at the time of survey. Furthermore, more than 50.0 per cent of them have loan outstanding upto Rs.2000/-. Like beneficiary household, non-beneficiary households have also borrowed. While 62.50 per cent of the non-beneficiary households have borrowed, more than 50.0 per cent of them have loan upto Rs.2000/-.

Comparing between different regions it can be observed that both in north and south regions almost all the beneficiary households have borrowed, though only 97.50 per cent have borrowed in the central region (Table 5.8). The share of borrowed non-beneficiary households, however, are lower than beneficiary households in all the different regions. But the share of non-beneficiary borrowers is highest in the south region (63.64 per cent) and lowest in the north region (60.0 per cent).

The average loan outstanding of beneficiary households is about Rs.4673 (Table 5.9). The average loan outstanding of non-beneficiary households is though lower than beneficiary households, yet it is quite severe and it seems difficult for them to repay out of their income. The situation is more severe in south region in the case of beneficiary households. On the other hand, it appears to be more critical in central region in the case of non-beneficiary households. In these regions the average loan outstanding per borrower is more than the other regions. While average amount of loan outstanding of the beneficiary households is comparable with the non-beneficiary households in the central region and the north region, that of the non-beneficiary households is comparable with the beneficiary households in the central region and south region.

Table 5.9 also shows that 72.0 per cent of the sample beneficiary households have brought loan from informal sector alone. In contrast to this about 96.0 per cent of non-beneficiary households have brought loan from informal sector. The share of loan out of the total borrowed loan from informal sector is also too high: about 69.0 per cent in the case of beneficiary households and about 86.0 per cent in the case of non-beneficiary households. It is to be noted that the rate of interest in the informal sector is five times higher than that of the formal sector. On account of the failure of formal credit institutions to supply credit to meet the requirement of both beneficiary and non-beneficiaries, the borrowers are forced to borrow credit at a higher rate of interest from informal credit agencies. Hence, it is an over burden on thepart of sample households which lead them into debt trap.

The higher share of beneficiary households taking loan from informal sector is observed in the north region, with the lowest share in the central region. On the other hand, in the case of non-beneficiary households, none of the borrowers has taken loan from formal sector, though one household in south region has taken loan from both formal and informal sectors and hence, they depend on informal sector. This might be due to the reluctance of the formal sector institutions for providing loan to the non-beneficiary households.

It can be seen from Table 5.9 that the purpose of taking loan is more for consumption than for income generating activities. The purpose of taking loan for ceremonial activities is also observed to be high. This is observed both in the case of beneficiary and non-beneficiary households in all the regions. Hence, more and more loan for consumption purpose would bring the sample households into debt trap. This portrays the situation of hunger in the Bengunia Block.

Literacy

It can be observed from Table 5.10 that the literacy rate of the sample beneficiary households (65.28 per cent) in the block is higher than the sample non-beneficiary households (41.0 per cent). The literacy rate of the beneficiary households is higher than the block average (53.71 per cent) as well as the state average (49.09 per cent). On the other hand, the literacy rate of non-beneficiary households is not only lower than the beneficiary households, but also lower than the block and state averages. The lower performance of non-beneficiary households compared to the beneficiary households in respect of literacy might be due to the extreme poverty and hunger in the case of the former than the latter. Besides the overall literacy, the literacy rate of both males and females in the case of non-beneficiary households is lower as compared to the sample beneficiaries. Even it is lower compared to the block average. This indicates that literacy campaign has not provided much benefit to the non-beneficiaries in the block.

The lower level of male and female literacy in the case of non-beneficiaries as compared to the beneficiaries is also observed in all the different regions. However, inter-regional comparison of literacy shows that central region has a lower performance regarding both male and female literacy compared to other regions. This is true in the case of both beneficiaries and non-beneficiaries. The lower performance of literacy in central region might be due to the fact that the number of schools in this region is lower than other regions. Furthermore, central region is very near to Khurda, where there is ample educational facilities. Even though, most of the offices are situated here, yet the employees and elites residing in Begunia might be interested for sending their children to Khurda, where they get better educational facilities.

It is interesting to observe that the literacy rate is more in the lower age group i.e. below 15 years, than in the higher age groups, i.e.15 to 50 years and above. This is observed both in the case of beneficiary household and non-beneficiary households. However, the literacy rate is lower in the case of non-beneficiaries compared to the beneficiaries in all the different age groups (Table 5.10). This is also found to be true in the different regions. Inter-regionally it is found that the performance of literacy in the age group below 15 years is better in the north region in the case of beneficiaries and in the south region in the case of non-beneficiaries.

The literacy rate of about 70.0 per cent in the case of beneficiaries and 35.0 per cent in the case of non-beneficiaries in the age group 15 to 50 years show that the adult literacy campaign has not benefited much to the non-beneficiaries compared to the beneficiaries. The severity is observed in the south region, where only 29.31 per cent of the non-beneficiaries are literate compared to 71.75 per cent of the beneficiaries in the age group 15 to 50 years.

As can be seen from Table 5.11, in the age group of below 15 years, a significant proportion of literates has taken formal education i.e. gone to school. The formal education among girls and boys is found to be satisfactory. However, it is interesting to observe that the percentage share of schooling in total literates among girls (below 15 years) in the case of non-beneficiaries is higher than the beneficiaries. This might be due to the fact that the sample of non-beneficiary households (40) is too low compared to the beneficiary households (200). Hence, there is every possibility that the result might be biased. Therefore, this can be considered as exceptional. The high level of formal education can have the potential to increase their access to information which ultimately help them in both rural farm and non-farm sector.

Region-wise it is observed that the percentage share of schooling in total literates is more in the case of non-beneficiaries than the beneficiaries in the central and north regions. This again might be due to the lower sample of non-beneficiaries compared to beneficiaries.

Health Facility

Table 5.12 shows the poor health care of both sample beneficiary and non-beneficiary households in the block. Even though 92.50 per cent of sample beneficiary households and the same percentage of non-beneficiary households go to Government health centres for their primary health care, they are not satisfied with medical facilities provided to them. More than 92.0 per cent of sample beneficiaries and 83.0 per cent of non-beneficiaries who are going to health centres claim that they are not getting common medicines adequately. This compels them to purchase such medicines from private stores at a higher price.

Even though there is health facilities, most of the sample households have to depend on private treatment even for minor diseases. This is observed in the case of about 68.0 per cent of beneficiaries and 70.0 per cent of non-beneficiaries. Due to this the sample households have to spend more on health care. It is observed that about 35.0 per cent of beneficiary households and 25.0 per cent of non-beneficiary households are suffering from serious diseases (Table 5.12). This is the non-calorie indicator of poverty and seems to be severe leading to hunger. This happens despite the huge expenditure on health by the State Government.

It is interesting to observe that even though in the south region health facility is better compared to other regions, the share of beneficiaries going to government hospitals is lower than other regions in the case of both beneficiaries and non-beneficiaries. This might be due to the fact that many times government doctors are remaining absent in the headquarters. Furthermore, due to large coverage of the south region, the patients do not like to be treated in the government health centres and instead depend on local treatment. Furthermore, percentage share of sample households suffering form serious diseases is more in the south region than in other regions both in the cases of beneficiaries and non-beneficiaries. This indicates that providing health centres only will not solve the problem of poor. They need more access to health services that the mere provision of health centres in order to be freed from hunger.

Drinking Water Facility

Both the beneficiary and non-beneficiary households mostly depend on tubewells and wells for drinking water. But the dependence is more on wells than on tubewells (Table 5.13). Since the wells are open and the disinfectants are rarely used, they have to take impure water. The less dependence on tubewell is due to the lower number of tubewells on the one hand and non-repair of existing non-functioning tubewells, on the other. Furthermore, availability of ground water at a deep level from the surface also prevents both beneficiary and non-beneficiary to depend on tubewell. This indicates that the authorities responsible for this have not taken much interest for providing safe drinking water facility in the area. Furthermore, the sample households do not get adequate drinking water during the peak summer. This might be due to the fact that ground water is available at a very deep level from the surface. The problem is more acute in the south region as compared to other regions, which might be due to the fact that the south region is situated at a higher level as compared to other regions. At the same time stone layers are found in the south region which might be preventing to dig deeper wells.

Dwelling Status

The dwelling status of the sample households is not found to be satisfactory. About 6.0 per cent of beneficiary households and 15.0 per cent of non-benefficiary households do not have the house on their own lands (Table 5.14). About 2.5 per cent of the beneficiary households got assistance from Government to construct their houses. The remaining 97.5 per cent are forced to meet the expenses the expenses for constructing the houses by their own effort.

It is observed that about 90.0 per cent of the beneficiary household in the Bengunia Block have *kutcha* houses with thatched roof. In contrast almost all the non-beneficiary households live in such houses in the block (Table 5.14). Houses having Khaparali, tile and asbestos roofs are rare in the block.

The *kutcha* houses both in the case of beneficiary and non-beneficiary households are not repaired and renovated regularly due to paucity of funds. The old thatches are again not removed regularly by never once both by beneficiary and non-beneficiary households although the problem is more acute in the case of the latter. Besides, their houses are of small in size, which forces them to live in congested spaces.

However, the variation is not in respect of dwelling status of the beneficiary and non-beneficiary households in different region.

Sanitation and Electricity Facility

Besides the poor dwelling status, the sanitation and electricity facilities of the sample households are not found to be satisfactory. Only 4 per cent of the beneficiary household and none of the non-beneficiary households have independent latrine in their house (Table 5.15). Hence, almost all the sample households use open latrine. Compared between different regions, it is observed that while in the central region none of the beneficiary households has independent latrine, in the north region about 6 per cent and in the south about 4.55 per cent have got independent latrines.

About 10.5 per cent of the beneficiary households and 2.5 per cent of the non-beneficiary households have legally connected electricity to their houses (Table 5.15). This lower share is mostly due to their poor economic condition. Some households get electric connection illegally and this creates a huge loss for the government in terms of revenue. Region-wise it can be noticed that the percentage of beneficiaries legally connecting electricity is highest in the central region (17.50 per cent), followed by north region (14.0 per cent) and south region (6.36 per cent). On the other hand, the legal connection of electricity in the case of non-beneficiaries is found only in the south region.

Table 5.1

Social Composition of Sample Beneficiairies and Non-Beneficiaries

Sl. No.	*Regionq*	*Status*	*Family Size*	*No. of Households*				
				S.C.	*S.T.*	*OBC*	*GENERAL*	*TOTAL*
1.	Central	Beneficiary	5.62	23 (57.5)	3 (7.5)	8 (20.0)	6 (15.0)	40 (100.0)
		Non-Beneficiary	3.12	2 (25.0)	3 (37.5)	3 (37.5)	0	8 (100.0)
2.	North	Beneficiary	5.14	11 (22.0)	11 (22.0)	16 (32.0)	12 (24.0)	50 (100.0)
		Non-Beneficiary	4.3	1 (10.0)	4 (40.0)	3 (30.0)	2 (20.0)	10 (100.0)
3.	South	Beneficiary	5.80	28 (25.5)	23 (20.9)	41 (37.3)	18 (16.4)	110 (100.0)
		Non-Beneficiary	4.2	6 (27.3)	8 (36.4)	5 (22.7)	3 (13.6)	22 (100.0)
4.	All (Block)	Beneficiary	5.60	62 (31.0)	37 (18.5)	65 (32.5)	36 (18.0)	200 (100.0)
		Non-Beneficiary	4.0	9 (22.5)	15 (37.5)	11 (27.5)	5 (12.5)	40 (100.0)

Note: Figures in the parentheses are percentage share of total households.
Source: Compiled from Field Data.

Table 5.2

Region-wise Agricultural Condition of Sample Households

Sl. No.	*Region*	*Status of households*	*No. of Labour Households*	*No. of cultivator* households	*Avg. size of land* holding (in AC)	*Area irrigated land* (AC)	*No. of leased out* households	*Area of leased* in land
1.	Central	Beneficiary	15 (37.50)	25 (62.50)	1.61	9.25 (22.92)	4 (16.0)	9.96 (22.58)
		Non-Beneficiary	7 (87.50)	1 (12.50)	0.50	-	-	1.80 (78.26)
2.	North	Beneficiary	19 (38.0)	31 (62.0)	2.20	1.55 (2.28)	5 (16.13)	15.15 (21.28)
		Non-Beneficiary	9 (90.0)	1 (10.0)	0.18	-	-	--

(Contd...)

Table 5.2 (Contd)...

Region-wise Agricultural Condition of Sample Households

Sl. No.	*Region*	*Status of households*	*No. of Labour Households*	*No. of cultivator households*	*Avg. size of land holding (in AC)*	*Area irrigated land (AC)*	*No. of leased out households*	*Area of leased*
3.	South	Beneficiary	32 (29.09)	78 (70.91)	1.28	16.14 (16.11)	6 (7.69)	64.91 (41.65)
		Non-Beneficiary	19 (86.36)	3 (13.64)	0.57	--	-	1.50 (46.58)
4.	All	Beneficiary	66 (33.00)	134 (67.0)	1.56	26.94 (12.92)	15 (11.19)	90.02 (33.20)
		Non-Beneficiary	35 (87.50)	5 (12.5)	0.48	--	--	3.30 (57.89)

Note: (a) Figures in brackets of col. 4 & 5 arepercentage share in total households.
(b) Figures in brackets of col. 7 are percentage share in total Agricultural land.
(c) Figures in brackets of col.8 are percentage share in total cultivator households.
(b) Figures in brackets of col. 9 are percentage share in total operational land.

Source: Compiled from Field Data.

Table 5.3

Distribution of Sample House Holds on The Basis of Their Value (In Rs.) of Assets

Sl. No. (1)	*Region* (2)	*Status of Households* (3)	*Up to 5000* (4)	*5000-10,000* (5)	*10,000-15,000* (6)	*15,000-20,000* (7)	*20,000-25,000* (8)	*Above 25,000* (9)	*Total* (0)
1.	Central	Beneficiary	6	5	3	1	5	20	40
			(15.0)	(12.5)	(7.50)	(2.50)	(12.50)	(50.0)	(100.0)
		Non-Beneficiaries	6	1	-	-	-	1	8
			(75.0)	(12.5)	-	-	-	(12.5)	
2.	North	Beneficiary	9	4	2	9	4	22	50
			(18.0)	(8.0)	(4.0)	(18.0)	(8.0)	(4.0)	(100.0)
		Non-Beneficiary	5	4	1	-	-	-	10
			(50.0)	(40.0)	(10.0)	-	-	-	(100.0)
3.	South	Beneficiary	11	9	15	14	8	53	110
			(10.0)	(8.18)	(13.64)	(12.73)	(7.27)	(48.18)	(100.0)
		Non-Beneficiary	11	5	3	2	1	-	22
			(50.0)	(22.73)	(13.64)	(9.09)	(4.54)	-	(100.0))
4.	All	Beneficiary	26	198	20	24	17	95	200
			(13.0)	(9.0)	(10.0)	(12.0)	(8.50)	(47.50)	(100.0)
		Non-Beneficiary	22	10	4	2	1	1	40
			(55.0)	(25.0)	(10.0)	(5.0)	(2.5)	(2.5)	(100.0)

Note: Figures in the parentheses are percentage share of total.
Source: Compiled from Field Data.

Table 5.4

Value of Different Assets Possessed by Average Sample household (In Rs.)

Si. No.	Region	Status of Households	Total Assets	Household Assets	Bovine Population	Trees& Plants	Durable Assets	Land & Farm Imple- ments	Non-Farm Imple- ment	Financial Assets	Other Assets
(1)	(2)	(3)	(4)	(5)	(6)	(7)	(8)	(9)	(0)	(11)	(12)
1.	Central	Beneficiary	34845.75	16340.75	858.75	937.50	916.25	13445	1277.50	890	180
			(100.0)	(46.89)	(2.46)	(2.69)	(2.63)	(38.58)	(3.67)	(2.55)	(0.52)
		Non-Bene-	9825	5962.50	700	137.50	225	2800	--	--	--
		ficiary	(100.00)	(42.37)	(7.12)	(1.40)	(2.29)	(28.50)	--	--	--
2.	North	Beneficiary	43239	18319	954	1716	1629	20202	326	644	49
			(100.0)	(42.37)	(2.21)	(3.97)	(2.38)	(46.72)	(0.75)	(1.49)	(0.11)
		Non-Bene-	4049	3799	60	140	50	--	--	--	--
		ficiary	(100.00)	(93.83)	(1.48)	(3.46)	(1.23)	--	-	--	--
3.	South	Beneficiary	34619.73	14606.36	803.64	1729.73	828.18	15861.23	138.32	652.27	--
			(100.00)	(42.19)	(2.32)	(5.00)	(2.39)	(45.82)	(0.40)	(1.88)	--
		Non-Bene-	6827.27	4847.72	95.45	218.18	40.91	1625	--	--	-
		ficiary	(100.00)	(71.01)	(1.40)	(3.20)	(0.60)	(23.80)	--	--	--
4.	All	Beneficiary	36819.75	15881.40	852.25	1567.85	896	16463.17	413.70	697.75	48.25
			(100.00)	(43.13)	(2.31)	(4.26)	(2.43)	(44.71)	(1.12)	(1.90)	(0.13)
		Non-Bene-	6732.25	4808.50	207.50	182.50	80	1453.75	--	--	--
		ficiary	(100.00)	(71.42)	(3.08)	(2.71)	(1.19)	(21.59)	--	--	--

Note: Figure in the parentheses are perccentage share of total.
Source: Compiled from Field Data

Table 5.5

Average Annual Income of Sample Households in Different Regions of Begunia Block (In Rs.)

Sl. No.	*Region*	*Status of Households*	*Agriculture*	*Allied To Agr.*	*Non-Farm*	*Wage Income*	*Remmittances*	*Transfer Payment*	*Others*	*Total*
(1)	(2)	(3)	(4)	(5)	(6)	(7)	(8)	(9)	(10)	(11)
1.	Central	Beneficiary	2397.00	439.05	1315.60	4134.37	1605.00	561.60	2054.75	12,507.40
			(19.17)	(3.51)	(10.52)	(33.06)	(12.83)	(4.49)	(16.43)	(100.00)
		Non-Bene-	362.50	325.00	--	1995.00	---	--	725.00	3,407.50
		ficiary	(10.64)	(9.54)	--	(58.55)	--	--	(21.28)	(100.00)
2.	North	Beneficiary	2924.50	353.40	526.60	3147.20	1566.00	528.00	1884.40	10,930.10
			(26.76)	(3.23)	(4.82)	(28.79)	(14.33)	(4.83)	(17.24)	(100.00)
		Non-Bene-	70.00	--	570.00	3480.00	50.00	--	60.00	4,680.00
		ficiary	(1.50)	--	(12.78)	(74.36)	(1.07)	--	(1.28)	(100.00)
3.	South	Beneficary	2569.22	456.18	779.32	3793.86	752.73	229.09	2665.00	11,240.85
			(22.86)	(4.06)	(6.93)	(33.75)	(6.70)	(2.04)	(23.71)	(100.00)
		Non-bene	135.50	--	246.82	4178.41	186.36	--	609.09	5,356.18
		ficiary	(2.53)	--	(4.61)	(78.01)	(3.48)	--	(11.37)	(100.00)
4.	All	Beneficiary	2623.60	426.06	823.39	3700.30	1126.50	370.32	2347.80	11,418.97
			(22.98)	(3.74)	(7.21)	(32.40)	(9.87)	(3.24)	(20.56)	(100.00)
		Non-Bene	164.52	65.00	278.25	3567.13	227.50	--	495.00	4,797.40
		ficiary	(3.43)	(1.35)	(5.80)	(74.36)	(4.74)	--	(10.32)	(100.00)

Note: Figure in the parentheses are percentage share of total income.
Source: Compiled from Field Data.

Table 5.6

Average Annual Expenditure of Sample Households in Different Regions of Begunia Block (In Rs.)

SL. No.	Region	Status of Households	Food: Cereals	Food: Total	Clothing	Health	Edu-cation	House Repairing	Care-monials	Others	Total
(1)	(2)	(3)	(4)	(5)	(6)	(7)	(8)	(9)	(10)	(11)	(12)
1.	Central	Beneficiary	6276.72	9965.82	1357.50	584.25	397.00	689.00	847.50	351.25	14,192.32
			(44.23)	(70.22)	(9.57)	(4.12)	(2.80)	(4.85)	(5.97)	(2.47)	(100.00)
		Non-Ben-ficiary	3421.25	4351.62	318.75	115.00	62.50	206.25	181.25	62.50	5,297.87
			(64.58)	(82.14)	(6.02)	(2.17)	(1.18)	(3.89)	(3.42)	(1.18)	(100.00)
2.	North	Beneficiary	5061.60	8004.28	1204.00	633.00	425.60	524.50	420.00	301.00	11,322.38
			(44.66)	(69.53)	(10.46)	(5.49)	(3.70)	(4.56)	(3.65)	(2.61)	(100.00)
		Non-Bene-ficiary	4081.00	4890.00	445.00	270.00	70.00	180.00	73.50	255.00	6183.50
			(66.00)	(79.08)	(7.20)	(4.37)	(1.13)	(2.91)	(1.19)	(4.12)	(100.00)
3.	South	Beneficiary	6177.29	9260.99	1240.45	723.54	391.73	603.64	552.73	413.73	13,186.81
			(46.84)	(70.34)	(9.36)	(5.01)	(3.14)	(4.69)	(4.70)	(2.75)	(100.00)
		Non-Bene-ficiary	4156.00	5229.13	465.91	1267.27	104.55	290.91	129.55	96.00	7,583.25
			(54.80)	(68.96)	(6.14)	(16.71)	(1.38)	(3.84)	(1.71)	(1.27)	(100.00)
4.	All	Beneficiary	5918.25	9087.78	1254.75	673.04	401.25	600.93	578.50	373.05	12,969.30
			(45.63)	(70.07)	(9.67)	(5.19)	(3.09)	(4.63)	(4.46)	(2.88)	(100.00)
		Non-Bene-ficiary	3990.30	4968.85	431.25	787.50	87.50	246.25	125.88	129.05	6,776.28
			(58.89)	(73.33)	(6.36)	(11.62)	(1.29)	(3.64)	(1.86)	(1.90)	(100.00)

Note: Figures in the parentheses are percentage share of Total Expenditure.
Source: Compiled from Field Data.

Table 5.7

Annual Consumption of Cereals

Zone	*Beneficiary*			*Non-Beneficiary*		
	Total Households consumption per Annum (in kg)	*Percapita per Annum (in Kg)*	*Percapita per day (in gram)*	*Total Households consumption per annum* (in kg)	*Percapita per annum (in kg)*	*Percapita per day (in gram)*
Central	875.48	159.70	444	485.63	178.72	496
North	708.26	147.76	410	589.00	189.40	526
South	889.73	158.24	440	669.55	158.30	440
All (Block)	841.51	155.91	433	612.63	170.16	473

Source: Compiled from Field Data..

Table 5.8

No. of Sample Households Having Loan Out Standing in Different Regions of the Begunia Block

Region	*% of share of Households having loan outstanding*		*Upto 1000*		*Rs.1000-2000*		*Rs. 2000-5000*		*Rs. 5000-10,000*		*Above 10,000*		*Total*	
	(B)	(N)	(B)	(N)	(B)	(N)	(B)	(N)	(B)	(N)	(B)	(N)	(B)	(N)
Central	97,50	62.50	9 (23.08)	1 (20.0)	13 (33.33)	-	9 (23.08)	2 (40.0)	8 (20.51)	2 (40.0)	--	--	39 (100.0)	5 (100.0)
North	100.0	60.0	14 (28.0)	3 (50.6)	15 (30.0)	-- --	15 (30.0)	3 (50.0)	1 (2.0)	-- --	5 (10.0)	-- --	50 (100.0)	6 (100.0)
South	100.0	63.64	19 (17.27)	4 (28.57)	34 (30.91)	6 (42.86	31 (28.18)	2 (14.29)	13 (11.82)	1 (7.14)	14 (12.73)	1 (5.88)	110 (100.0)	14 (100.0)
All	99.50	62.50	42 (21.11)	8 (32.00)	62 (31.16)	6 (24.0)	54 (27.14)	7 (28.0)	22 (11.06)	3 (12.0)	19 (9.55)	1 (4.0)	199 (100.0)	25 (100.0)

Note: (1) Figure in Brackets are percentage share of total.

(2) B=Beneficiary households and N=Non-beneficiary houeholds.

Source: Compiled from Field Data.

Table 5.9

Average Loan Oustanding, Loan from Different Sectors

Region	Average Loan out standing (Rs.)	No. of persons taking loan from different sector: Formal	Informal	Both	Total	Share of Loan (%): Formal	Informal	Rate of interest per annum(%): Formal	informal	Purpose of loan: a	b	c	d	all
1. Benefiicary														
Central	3679.50	5	26	8	39	25.67	74.93	12	60	8	19	12	1	40
		(12.82)	(66.67)	(20.51)	(100.00)									
North	3809.20	4	40	6	50	12.63	87.37	12	60	11	24	10	4	49
		(8.00)	(80.00)	(12.00)	(100.00)									
South	5385.36	7	78	25	110	38.61	61.39	12	60	30	50	15	11	106
		(6.36)	(70.91)	(22.73)	(100.00)									
All	4673.52	16	144	39	199	31.15	68.85	12	60	49	93	37	16	195
		(8.04)	(72.36)	(19.60)	(100.00)									
2. Non-Beneficiary														
Central	4400.00	-	5	-	5	0.0	100.00	-	60	-	2	2	1	5
			(100.00)		(100.00)									
North	2266.67	-	6	-	6	0.0	100.00	-	60	-	3	2	1	6
			(100.00)		(100.00)									
South	4392.86	-	13	1	14	13.82	86.18	12	60	1	11	1	1	14
			(92.86)	(7.14)	(100.00)									
All	3884.00	-	24	1	25	8.75	91.25	12	60	1	16	5	3	25
					(96.0)	(4.0)	(100.00)							

Notes: Figure in the parenthesis are percentage share of total.

* Considering all the households

a = Income generating activities, b = Consuption, c = Ceremonies/rituals, d = health/medical treatment.

Source: Compiled from Field Data.

Table 5.10

Percentage Share of Literates of the beneficiaries in Different Regions of the Begunia Block

Zone	*Below 15 Years*			*15 to 50 Years*			*Above*			*Total*		
	Male	*Female*	*Total*	*Male*	*Female*	*Total*	*Male*	*Female*	*Total*	*Male*	*Female*	*Total*
Central	69.44 (40.00)	76.47 (-)	71.70 (22.22)	83.33 (50.0)	51.61 (33.33)	67.21 (40.0)	70.59 (-)	29.41 (-)	50.00 (-)	76.99 (30.77)	47.17 (16.67)	62.56 (24.0)
North	92.00 (60.00)	88.23 (72.73)	90.48 (61.54)	79.45 (57.14)	52.54 (42.86)	67.42 (47.62)	81.25 (25.0)	52.38 (-)	66.67 (16.67)	85.45 (50.0)	50.44 (45.83)	66.81 (47.50)
South	94.74 (66.67)	64.18 (72.73)	78.23 (69.23)	88.96 (29.63)	53.29 (29.03)	71.75 (29.3)	68.75 (66.67)	21.92 (25.0)	43.80 (47.06)	85.56 (47.06)	47.94 (38.0)	66.49 (42.57)
All	86.44 (60.0)	70.30 (56.52)	79.00 (58.33)	85.47 (36.84)	52.75 (33.33)	69.77 (34.83)	71.88 (41.18)	28.83 (16.67)	48.79 (31.0)	83.14 (45.0)	50.93 (37.21)	65.28 (40.96)

Note: Figures in the parentheses are percentage share of literates among non-beneficiaries
Source: Compiled from the Field Data

Table 5.11

Percentage Share of Schooling to total Literates in the cas of beneficiaries in Different Regions of Begunia Block

Zone	*Below 15 Years*			*15 to 50 Years*			*Above*			*Total*		
	Male	*Female*	*Total*	*Male*	*Female*	*Total*	*Male*	*Female*	*Total*	*Male*	*Female*	*Total*
Central	96.00 (100.00)	92.31 (0.0)	94.74 (100.0)	10.00 (0.0)	9.38 (0.0)	9.76 (0.0)	0.00 (0.0)	0.00 (0.0)	0.00 (0.0)	33.33 (50.0)	30.00 (0.0)	32.12 (33.33)
North	95.45 (66.67)	80.00 (100.0)	86.84 (87.50)	10.34 (0.0)	9.68 (16.67)	10.12 (10.0)	0.00 (0.0)	0.00 (0.0)	0.00 (0.0)	28.72 (25.0)	26.37 (54.55)	27.81 (42.11)
South	96.30 (70.0)	81.40 (87.50)	89.69 (77.78)	26.21 (12.5)	28.40 (0.0)	26.99 (5.88)	11.36 (0.0)	6.25 (0.0)	10.00 (0.0)	39.09 (33.33)	42.41 (36.84)	40.21 (34.88)
All	95.10 (73.33)	71.83 (92.31)	90.17 (82.14)	19.37 (7.14)	20.14 (5.88)	19.65 (6.45)	7.25 (0.6)	3.13 (0.0)	5.94 (0.0)	35.61 (33.33)	36.03 (40.62)	35.77 (36.76)

Note: Figures in the parentheses are percentage share of schooling to total literates in the case of non-beneficiaries.
Source: Compiled from Field Data.

Table 5.12

Health Facilities of Sample Beneficiaries and Non-Beneficiaries

Zone	*Beneficiaries*				*Non-Beneficiaries*			
	Depend upon Govt. Hospitals	*Prescribed medicines not gett-ing from hospital*	*Private treat-ment diseases*	*Suffer-ing from serious diseases*	*Depend upon Govt. Hos-pital*	*Prescri-bed medi-ines notment getting from hospitq*	*Private treatement for severe disease*	*Suffer-ing from severe diseases*
Centr	40 (100.00)	40 (100)	37 (92.50)	13 (32.50)	8 (100.00)	8 (100.0)	8 (100.0)	2 (25.00)
North	47 (94.00)	46 (97.87)	43 (86.00)	15 (30.00)	10 (100.00)	9 (90.0)	8 (80.00)	2 (26.00)
South	98 (89.09)	85 (86.76)	56 (50.91)	41 (37.27)	19 (86.36)	14 (73.68)	12 (54.55)	6 (27.27)
All	185 (92.50)	171 92.43)	136 (68.00)	69 (34.50)	37 (92.50)	31 (83.78)	28 (70.00)	10 (25.00)

Note: Figures in the parentheses are percentage share in the total sample beneficiaries, and total sample non-beneficiaries.
Source: Compiled from the Field Data.

Table 5.13

Drinking Water Facility of Beneficiaries and Non-beneficiaries in different regions of the block (In No.)

Zone	*Beneficiaries*				*Adequacy of drinking water during summer*	*Non-Beneficiaries*				*Adequacy of drinking water during summer*
	a	*b*	*c*	*d*		*a*	*b*	*c*	*d*	
Central	-	23	33	11	21 (52.50)	-	2	6	1	4 (50.0)
north	-	33	24	1	32 (64.00)	-	6	4	-	7 (70..0)
South	2	34	78	2	79 (71.82)	-	8	15	-	17 (77.27)
All	2	90	135	3	102 (51.00)	-	16	25	1	28 (70.00)

Note : i) a = piped water
b = tubewell
c = well
d = other

ii) Figures in the parentheses are percentage share of total.

Source: Compiled from Field data.

Table 5.14

Dwelling Status of Sample Households in Different Regions of the Begunia Block

Region	Status	Percentage of Beneficiary HHs having no house on their own land	Percentage of beneficiary got asst. for constructing house	Structure of the House (Nos) No. of total HHs	Pucca with RC	Pucca without RC	Kutch a	b	c	d	Total
Central	Beneficiary	5.00	-	40 (100.00)	2 (5.0)	3 (7.50)	-	-	34	1	35 (87.50)
	Non-Beneficiary	37.50	-	8 (100.00)	-	-	-	-	8	-	8 (100.0)
North	Beneficiary	8.00	10.00	50 (50.00)	2 (4.0)	2 (4.0)	--	--	43	3	46 (92.0)
	Non-Beneficiary	10.00	-	10 (100.0)	-	-	-	-	10	-	10 (100.0)

(Contd...)

Table 5.14 (Contd...)

Dwelling Status of Sample Households in Different Regions of the Begunia Block

Region	Status	Percentage of Benefici ary HHs hav-ing no house on their own land	Percentage of benefici-ary got asst. for constructing house	Structure of the House (Nos)			Kutch				
				No. of total	Pucca with RC	Pucca without RC	a	b	c	d	Total
South	Beneficiary	5.45.	-	110 (100.0)	5 (4.54)	4 (3.64)	-	4	94	3	101 (91.82)
	Non Beneficiary	9.09	-	22 (100.0)	--	--	--	--	22	-	22 (100.0)
All	Beneficiary	6.00	2.50	200 (100.0)	9 (4.50)	9 (4.50)	-	4	171	7	182 (91.0)
	Non-Beneficiary	15.00	- 40	- (100.0)	-	--	-	40	-	40	(100.0)

Notes: (i) a= Khaparali, b= tile, c= thatched, d= asbestos.

(ii) Figures in the parentheses are percentage share of total households.

Source: Compiled from Field Data.

Table 5.15

Sanitary & Power facilities of the sample Households in different Region of Begunia Block

Zone	*Sanitary Faciliites*		*Power Facilities*	
	Beneficiaries Independent Latrine	*Non - Baneficiaries Independent Latrine*	*Beneficiaries legally connected with electricity*	*Non-Beneficiaries legally connected with electricity*
Central	--	--	7 (17.50)	--
North	3 (6.00)	--	7 (14.00)	--
South	5 (4.55)	--	7 (6.36)	1 (4.55)
All	8 (4.00)	--	21 (10.50)	1 (2.50)

Note: Figures in the perentheses are percentage share of total sample beneficiary/non-beneficiary households in the respected regions.
Source: Compiled from Field Data.

6

Catalysts For Growth And Measures For Their Promotion

This chapter is divided into three parts. In the first part catalysts for growth in the Begunia block are identified, while measures to promote them are suggested in the second part. How to allocate resources in different growth sectors to promote them and the Prioritisation of their investment are discussed in the last part.

Identification of Catalysts for Growth

So far we have observed the poor performance of direct action programmes against hunger and poverty in the Begunia block. These direct short-term measures will, however, help in tacking the immediate problem of deprivation, if corrections can be made for the critical gaps and missing links that have been observed in their structure and implementation. But this can not sustain for long unless long-term. It is necessary that the economy must be growing so that it can provide impetus to the short-term programmes for alleviating hunger and poverty. Furthermore, the long-term development benefits the poor through trickle down effect. However, for the long-term development of an underdeveloped economy, it is necessary to identify the growth stimulating factors, where investment can be made to give a boost to the economy.

An attempt has been made here to identify the catalysts for growth in the Begunia block of Orissa. The following catalysts have the potential for long-term development of an underdeveloped economy, like Begunia Block.

(1) Irrigation

(2) Industry
  (i) Agro-based Industry
  (ii) Handloom Industry

(3) Activities Allied to Agriculture
  (i) Diary
  (ii) Pisciculture

(4) Credit Delivery

(5) Infrastructure
  (i) Power
  (ii) Transport and Communication

(6) Human Resource Development
  (i) Education
  (ii) Health

How these can act as catalysts for growth are discussed in the following.

(1) Irrigation

Irrigation is an essential input for agricultural development. It promotes agricultural development in several ways. The immediate impact is on the change of cropping pattern in agriculture. A shift from the production of unremunerative crops to the production of more high valued crops takes place on account of extensive use of irrigation. Irrigation also contributes towards increase in farm productivity. This is achieved through an increase in the area under double and multiple cropping, an increase in the intensity of cultivation and through the adoption of high yielding varieties responsive to irrigation and fertilizer. A dry region previously having low yielding crops and unstable yields, enjoys the privilege of a more stable and higher value of output with the introduction of irrigation (Mishra, 1990)[1]. Farm inputs like improved seeds, fertilizer and extension etc., contribute their due share in food production only when assured water is available in agriculture.

In Orissa a few studies have been made in the recent years highlighting the importance of irrigation in agricultural development. Among these studies conducted by ORG[2] (1984) on minor irrigation in Dhenkanal district, Satapathy[3] (1984) on major and medium irrigation projects in Cuttack district and WALMI[4] (1988) on Kuanria medium irrigation project deserve worth mentioning. Like wise, a study conducted by Mallik, Padhi and Meher[5] (1994) on different systems of irrigation in three districts of Orissa has shown the contribution of irrigation on improvement of agricultural production and farm employment irrespective of the systems of irrigation pursued in agricultural sector. However, they have identified the importance of medium and minor irrigation in promoting agricultural production in the state in general and the study area in particular.

An inter-state comparison of the role of irrigation in economic development reveals that irrigation and contributed much towards the development of food production and farm employment in states like Punjab and Haryana. The net irrigated area as a percentage of net sown area in Punjab and Haryana is 92.7 and 72.7 respectively in the year 1991. In contrast, Orissa has only 30.7 per cent of net area irrigated out of the total net sown area in the year under reference. During this period the all India average of net area irrigated to total net area sown was 33.3 per cent.

In Orissa, irrigation has definitely contributed towards agricultural develoment in developed districts like Sambalpur, Cuttack, Puri and Ganjam. Percentage share of net irrigated area to net sown area was 31.53, 45.69, 52.65 and 49.20 respectively, in the year 1988-89. This was much higher than the state average of 27.55 per cent in the said year. In dry areas, however, there is lack of adequate irrigation facilities. With widespread network of irrigation opportunities, agricultural production and productivity of these areas are sure to increase.

(2) Industrial Development

Industrialisation plays a critical role in the process of economic development and is considered as one of the basic policy objectives for development in most of the developing countries. Accordingly more emphasis is given for the development of small scale industries not only to increase employment opportunities but also to modernise the rural economy. It is further maintained that the solution to the economic maladies like poverty, unemployment, malnutrition and endemic deprivation lies in the rapid industrialisation. Emphasis on Industrialisation, however, does not relegate agricultural development to the background. What is emphasised here is a harmonious balance between agriculturel and industry in the context of economic development of a country. In making efforts towards industrialisation, industries that make use of available local resources-man and material need be given more emphasis. Besides, industrialisation must spread equally to all the regions for realising the goal of balanced regional development. The following two types of industries can act as catalysts for growth in rural areas of the state in general and Begunia block in particular.

(i) Agro-Based Industry

Agro-based industries have certain advantages. These industries generate employment opportunities on a large-scale and contribute significantly to the process of self-sustained growth. According to an estimate by the Food & Agricultural Organisation (FAO) these industries account for about half of the total value added and almost two thirds of the employment in the developing countries (Venkaiah, 1987)[6]. Agro-industries have a special significance in order to bring about smooth transition from traditional to modern industry. Furthermore, by increasing the agricultural income, these industries make farmers go in for innovation and new technique of production. It has been the experience of countries like Japan, Taiwan and Denmark that agro-industries give considerable fillip to farm productivity by encouraging the use of improved technology by farming community (Gupta, 1993)[7]. Agro-industries help to promote both forward and backward linkages in agriculture. Forward linkage takes place when a number of agro-based industries using agricultural raw materials are set up. Backward linkage is achieved when farmers undertake the use of new technique of production, better farm implements, improved seeds and fertilizer for increasing agricultural production and productivity.Besides, ago-industries also help to promote marketing, better credit use and infrastructure network. The development of ago-based industries, therefore, can play catalytic role in the development of rural economy.

(ii) Handloom Industry

Handloom is the well recognised traditional industry of Orissa for its highly artistic design, colour combination and durability. The industry provides sustainable employment to a large number of traditional weavers of Sambalpur, Bolangir, Cuttack and Berhampur through Weavers' Coorperative Societies. By the end of 1993-94, about 2.11 lakh persons were employed both in Handloom Cooperatives and Corporate Sectors in Orissa.[8] Furthermore, handloom industry is in a position to generate additional employment for one lakh of persons at an investment of Rs.70 crores only (Meher, 1992)[9]. Besides employment, contribution of this industry towards the total earnings of the secondary sector in the state during 1987-88 was 10.51 per cent. This was possible due to large-scale export of handloom products to overseas markets. The development of handloom sector in an organised manner is likely to eradicate large scale unemployment and underemployment in the state in general and the study area in particular.

(3) Activities Allied to Agriculture

Agriculture is no more confined to mere food production. It embraces a host of other activities allied to agriculture as well. These allied activities include; dairy, poultry, fishery, goatery and horticulture etc. In agriculture the number of small and marginal farmers are quite large. It is difficult for them to maintain their livelihood solely on crop production as the agricultural income always tends to be lower. In order to supplement their income and to maintain reasonable standard of living, the small and marginal farmers pursue several activities allied to agriculture a subsidiary occupation. In agriculturally prosperous states like Punjab, Haryana and Andhra Pradesh these farmers seem to be adopting various allied activities for earning income and gainful employment. In the underdeveloped Begunia block, one notices the presence of a large mass of small and marginal farmers, the majority of whom belong to the category of Scheduled Castes and Scheduled Tribes. Of the several allied activities, dairy and pisciculture have a large scope for development in the block providing subsidiary employment to marginal and small farmers, and landless agricultural labourers.

(i) Dairy Development

Apart from increasing the availability of milk products, dairing and rearing of milch animals have been considered as one of the activities aimed at alleviating endemic hunger and unemployment specially in rural areas. In the states like Punjab, Haryana, Rajasthan and Gujarat dairy development has been of great importance. In Orissa, on the other hand the development of dairy activities is slow and tary. As against the per capita milk productions of 269.0 kg 218.0 kg, 98.8 and 89.3 kg in Punjab, Harayana, Rajasthan and Gujarat respectively, Orissa has the per capita milk production of only 16.2 kg during 1992-93[10]. The development of dairy sector will not only increase the per capita milk production but agricultural families belonging to small and marginal farmers in the rural areas of Orissa. The success in this direction lies in providing better milch cows, effective veterinary services, cheap credit from credit agencies and supply of fodder to the needy farmers.

(ii) Pisciculture

Pisciculture is another important allied activity that provides suitable opportunities of employment and livelihood to a large numbers of poor families. This activity is now not confined to fishermen community only. Rural people belonging to other castes and communities have also adopted pisciculture as a subsidiary occupation for supplementing their scant income derived from agriculture. Pisciculture has thus contributed substantially towards reducing unemployment and underemployment in the farm sector.

Pisciculture has developed significantly in neighbouring states like Andhra Pradesh and West Bengal. Pond fishing is popular in the state of Andhra Pradesh. There, production of fish is so high that even it is exported to places like Bhubaneswar, Cuttack, and Berhampur in Orissa. Likewise, West Bengal has occupied a significant position so far as inland fish production is concerned. As against these states Orissa does not lack much in respect of fish production. During 1991, the state ranked sixth position at the all-India level in respect of inland fish production. The districts where the prospect for fist production is large are Cuttack, Puri, Balasore and Ganjam. Even Sambalpur and Bolangir districts too provide immense potentialities for fish production. Establishment of fish farms, supply of fish seed, nets and other accessories, training and guidance to fishermen will go a longway in increasing production of fish in the State.

(4) Credit Delivery

Credit is one of the catalysts that help families to engage themselves in income generating activities. Hunger is not a problem of inadequate supply of food. It is the lack of means for buying the available food. Employment creation and income generation are the fundamental requirements for overcoming hunger and malnutrition in the country. For this a wide network of credit agencies is needed to be set up to provide adequate and cheap credit to the poor. In India the credit institutions operating in the rural areas are; Cooperative Banks, Commercial Banks and Regional Rural Banks. Since no single agency can meet all the requirements of loans by the poor, a scheme of multi-agency system has been evolved to provide all possible credit required by the poor. The objective is to engage poor and deprived people of rural areas in gainful productive activities through liberal credit without the insistence of any security so that they can earn income which would help them to buy food and other requirements to overcome hunger (World Bank 1994)[11].

5. Infrastructure

Infrastructure as a catalyst of growth no clarification. Due to its neglect in the initial stage of development many developing countries have faced the problem of slow growth. On the other hand, countries where infrastructure has developed significantly, there economic development has accelerated leaps and bounds. The cases of Japan, South Korea, Thailand and Singapore are bright examples. Among the infrastructures networks, power, roads, transport and communication are the most important.

(i) Power

In the field of infrastructure, power occupies a strategic position. Power is useful for the development of agriculture and industry. Due to better power facilities, Punjab and Haryana in the north, Andhra Pradesh and Karnataka in the south have made significant progress in agriculture. Similarly Maharastra, Gujarat and Tamil Nadu are industrially more advanced due to better power position in these states. A large number of small and medium industries have come up in these states due to the availability of power.

In Orissa the power supply position is not discouraging. Due to systematic efforts made by the State Government, the supply position with regard to power has improved considerably. Even then, there is mismatch between generation, transmission and distribution of power in the state. As a result of this, while the urban areas have the benefit of receiving constant power supply, the rural areas still go without power for a considerable part of the year. Improvement in the power position, therefore, would help in developing the economy of the state and the rural areas in particular.

(ii) Transport and Communication

Like power, better roads, transport and communication facilities are other essential prerequisites for the development of our economy. With better road links, transport and communication facilities trade and commerce can be developed significantly. Furthermore, procurement of various inputs for agriculture and raw materials for industries is possible when there is wide-spread network of transport and communication facilities in the economy. States like Punjab, Haryana, Maharastra and Gujarat are considered as developed states because of the existence of improved transport and communication facilities in these states. These facilities help these states to tap markets for the sale of their products and this in turn help them to increase the income earning capacity of the producers and businessmen. In Orissa, distribution of transport and communication network is highly uneven. While coastal districts like Cuttack, Puri and Ganjam have better communication facilities, the inland districts substantially lag far behind these districts in this regard. Therefore, improvement in the transport and communication network in all areas of the state is required for a smooth development.

(6) Human Resource Development

In the process of economic development, Human Resource Development occupies a significant place. Education and Health which are the two important ingredients of Human Resource Development help to improve the quality of life of the people besides creating awareness among them. In order to promote education and health services as a part of human resource development, targeted intervention by the Government is very often suggested.

(i) Education

Education accelerates growth and improves earning potential of the people. It has considerable impact in reducing hunger as it makes poor people aware through supply of information and extension services about the benefit of several poverty alleviation programmes launched by the government. Besides, education makes people conscious about their health and nutritional requirement which go a longway in improving their quality of life. Education has further the merit of reducing fertility rate by making family planning measures more acceptable amongst the poor. The development of social sector like education in Kerala and Srilanka has made significant impact on alleviating poverty (Basu, 1995)[12]. In Kerala the percentage of literacy remains at 89.8 as against 52.1 at the all-India level as per 1991 census.Hence, education has great importance in alleviating poverty and hunger in a poor economy like Orissa.

(ii) Health

Health is one of the basic indicators of development. It is necessary that people should be healthy and active in order to participate in different development programmes. What is required here is to improve the nutritional status of the poor. Hunger is a health issue, because persistent malnutrition make people vulnerable to endemic disease and epidemic infections and condems them to unhealthy and unproductive lives (World Bank, 1994)[13]. The important requirement here is to impart health education to poor people. They need be educated to reduce fertility rate through family planning measures. In this connection, the education of women is of utmost important. More the women are educated, greater will be the chance of reducing maternal and infant mortality. Kerala and Srilanka have achieved better health standards compared to even the economically advanced states and countries repetitively due to effective health and family planning programmes (Basu, 1995)[14]. The state like Orissa also needs improvement in health standards through effective measures.

The above catalysts for growth have their relevance in an underdeveloped block like Begunia in Orissa. Improvement in these catalysts for growth are, therefore, needed for the overall development of the block. If the investment in these growth inducing factors could be made then the process of development in the Begunia factors would be speeded up. This would reduce poverty and hunger in the long run through the access to factors that increase the return on assets held by the poor (i.e. water, credit, etc. be available). According to Serageldin, access to assets for those who have no assets also means access to the factors that increase the return on assets that are held by the poor.[15]

The catalysts of growth so identified have the potential to reduce poverty and hunger in the block and, therefore, it necessitates their immediate execution. The measures that can be adopted for the effective use of catalysts in the process of development of Begunia economy are discussed in the following section.

II

MEASURES FOR DEVELOPMENT OF THE CATALYSTS

After identifying the catalysts for growth in the block an attempt has been made here to suggest measures for their development.

Irrigation

It has already been discussed that irrigation is one of the major catalysts for development of the Begunia block leading to increased productivity and employment. Development of irrigation improves poor men's participation in growth and thus reduces hunger. It is, therefore, necessary to suggest measures that would be most appropriate for the development of irrigation in the block.

There are two ways in which irrigation potential can be created in the block. One is minor irrigation like: Dugwell, Tubewell and minor canal in the short run, and the other is major/medium canal irrigation in the long run. We will discuss first how irrigation potential can be created in the short run and then in the long run.

The satellite survey shows that in the Begunia block ground water is plentily available. This can be effectively utilised to irrigate for cultivation in two ways: through dugwell and tubewell. Though dugwell can be created with lowest cost, this may not be feasible in Begunia block due to the availability of groundwater at a very deep level under the surface. On the other hand, tubewell can tap deep confined aquifers (through deep tubewell} as well as shallow aquifers (through shallow tubewell). Since satellite survey mentions that ground water is plentily available but at a very low level (except in the case of river bed), the deep tubewell can be very useful for irrigation purpose in the block. But the deep tubewells are costly and hence, are not suited to the poor farmers. Hence, this should be provided by the government and managed jointly by the farmers and the government.

Besides the ground water potential, irrigation can also be created in the block through river lift. Due to the presence of a number of springs (Jharanas) are some rivers in different gram panchayats irrigation potential can be created through lifting water from these jharanas or rivers. However, all the jharanas are not in good condition. Hence, there is a need to renovate these jharanas so as to utilise effectively these for irrigation purposes. The river lifts should be provided by the government and managed jointly by the government and the farmers. Besides this, irrigation potential can also be created by constructing small embankments and reservoirs. In the south Begunia, embankment can be constructed at Kadargadia, Haja bandha and Siju bandha in Kunjuri Grampanchayat. This can be able to irrigate about 500 acres of land. Reservoirs can be constructed at the Gobari river in Botalma and Maluguni river (earlier known as Mandakini) in Siko Grampanchayat. This will help in irrigating a good patch of land in these areas of south Begunia. In the north Begunia, a small reservoir on Jodi bandha can be constructed in Badaberana Grampanchayat.

In the long-run, irrigation potential can be created by major canals. Since Mahanadi is near to the block, water from Mahanadi river can be brought to Brutanga through pipe line and a dam can be constructed at that river. However, it is learnt that a step in this direction has been initiated by the World Bank but the progress is very slow. Irrigation can be made for the whole Begunia block through canal system from this dam. Though the supply of water is importent in the block, yet the management of the distribution of available water supply needs to receive utmost attention (Misra, 1997)[16].

Agro-Based Industry

Since a significant proportion of geographical area is devoted to cashew plantation, production of cashew can be used for cashew processing industries. The installation of cashew processing units is very much in demand in Dingar, Haza, Gadamanitri, Deuli and Kunjri G.P.s. in south region; and Begunia and Baghamari G.P.s in central region. The raw materials are also available plentily in these areas. The cashew processing industries in south and central regions can employ a large number of poor thereby reducing their poverty and hunger.

Besides the cashew processing industries, food processing industries like tomato sauce, chilli sauce etc., can be effectively installed in the Haza G.P. in south Begunia; Kantabada and Pongarsingh GPs in north Begunia; and Baghamari G.P. in central Begunia due to their huge vegetable production. Furthermore, rice and oil mills can be installed in the block as a significant proportion of area is devoted to food crops. These industries can absorb a significant number of workers.

Even though bamboos are plentily available in the south region, particularly in Routpada and Gadamanitri GPs, due to lack of skill these are not exploited. Hence, steps can be taken to install cane industries in these areas, which will help the scheduled caste people for gainful employment. Besides the above, palm rope making unit in Siko G.P. and Agarbati industry in Delhi G.P. would employ a number of workers from poor families in South Begunia. Furthermore, Bidi making industry can also be set up in Botalma G.P. in south Begunia. This will engage a large number of both male and female workers.

There is also scope for the development of sericulture in the Siko and Haza G.P.s in south Begunia. This can help a number of families to come out of hunger and poverty.

Handloom Industry

South Begunia is a suitable place for the development of handloom industries. There are a large number of families, involved in weaving in Routpada, Botalma, Durghapur and Siko G.P.s in south Begunia. The conditions of these families are not only poor but they also lack modern skill. Though there are two handloom cooperative societies functioning in Routpada, these are financially not sound so as to equip them with modern techniques of weaving. In order to eradicate hunger and poverty these families should be provided with proper training in modern techniques of weaving. Powerlooms should also be provided to them which will help a lot to improve their financial condition. The government can also plan to set up a textile industry so as to absorb a large number of weavers and other families. The importance of handloom sector in this area is also due to the fact that even some of the handloom products are exported to outside the state. On several occasions the weavers of the block have been invited by Government to participate in regional and national level trade fairs and the weavers are found to have taken active interest in participating in such national level exhibitions.

Dairy

South Begunia is a suitable place for dairy development. In this region, particularly in Haza, it can help to a number of families to come out of poverty and hunger. Due to the huge production of milk in this area OMFED has made arrangements to collect milk every day directly from the producers for purpose of use by its chilling plant located in Bhubaneswar. Installation of dairy units is, therefore, required in this area to help in eradicating hunger and poverty. A medium scale dairy unit in Haza is suggested for the benefit of the people in this area.

Another dairy unit can also be set up in Sarua G.P in central

Begunia. Sarua GP has a better location well connected by communication facilities. Marketing of products can be made in Khurda, Banki and Nayagarh besides other distant places. But the main problem is the lack of fodder. Hence, steps can be taken to develop fodder in these areas as fodder cultivation can be possible in certain parts of Begunia block on account of favourable soil conditions. The development of dairy units will employ a large number of workers of the area who are now employed and steeped in poverty.

Besides the development of fodder cultivation and setting up of dairy units, veterinary service should also be improved.

Pisciculture

Pond fishing is not well development in the Begunia block. Therefore, steps should be taken to popularise pond fishing. The fishermen in the block also require adequate training on modern pisciculture technique. Though Fish Farmers Development Agency is created in the district by the Central Government to develop ponds and tanks and impart training, the fish farmers in the block are not benefited much. Besides training, the poor fishermen should also be provided with adequate easy credit so that they will not be exploited by the middlemen. Better quality of fish seed should also be provided to them for more production of fish.

Credit for the Poor

The RRBS which are created as institutional innovation for the rural poor have not come out with any radically different policy or strategy to reach out to them. The RRBs have followed mainly the established security based lending and hence, their success as an institutional innovation appears to be of a limited nature only. Since their basic policy has remained same with other institutions like the cooperatives and the commercial banks, the outcome is in no way significantly different[17]. Therefore, the system/practice of considering individual as the borrowing unit when linked to security-based lending has failed to serve the rural poor.

A model of group-based lending is most appropriate in areas with high population density, landlessness, and a semi-urban or rural non-farm economy[18]. A rural bank of this type called 'Grameen Bank' is working most successfully in Bangladesh. The Grameen Bank is a public sector credit institution land its aim is to provide loans to the poor on a reasonable terms. The idea is to enable poor tobecome self-sufficient. A member of any households owing less than half an acre of cultivable land can avail himself of the services of the Grameen Bank. The workers of the bank actually search for poor people who need financial support but are too ignorant or different to seek Credit.[19]

Unlike the RRB of India, the Grameen Bank in Bangladesh lends to a group of self selected persons consisting of five to eight members who agree to form a group in which they guarantee to monitor each other. Such group lending helps to screen out risky borrowers, and creates group pressure to monitor and enforce the term of the loan. Group enforcement substitutes for collateral, which most poor people lack. The group is organised and trained by Grameen Bank workers[20].

This group-based lending in Bangladesh has been able to overcome the main problem of collateral and in the process could reach even the poorest of the poor quite successfully. Studies done on Grameen Bank tells us that the borrowers have improved their income, widened their asset base, moved steadily towards crossing the poverty line and towards a life of dignity and honour. Studies also tell us that the nutritional level in Grameen families is better than in non-Grameen families, the chiled mortality is lower in Grameen families than in non-Grameen families and that adoption of family planning practices is higher in Grameen families than in non-Grameen families. All studies again confirm the visible empowerment of women in Grameen families (World Bank, 1994)[21]. All these facts only add up to say that if we had changed our banking system the poor world have had a chance to change their lives.

The Grameen Bank model of the above type where group leading is given utmost emphasis can, therefore, be the most appropriate in an underdeveloped block like Begunia. Even though in the block a group scheme like DWCRA is in vogue, yet it is not due to initiative from Bank's side and there are a number of problems like marketing and others.

Transport and Communication

Most of the village roads in the block are *kutcha*, for which the people in the villages are facing a lot of problems during the rainy season. There is, therefore, the need for converting the kutcha roads into pucca road as early as possible. Besides, transport and communication facilities to the distant GPs and remote rural areas in the north and south regions of the block are not satisfactory. As for instance, Deuli Panchayat which is situated at a distance of 20 kilometres away from block-headquarters does not have adequate transport and communication facilities. The same is the case with Siko and Sagadabhanga GPs of south region and Pongarsingh and Kantabada of northern region. One notices casual movement of a private bus from the block headquater to these Panchayats only in the evening time. In the absence of trucks, tempos and trekkers plying between these Panchayats and the block headquarters, the movement of agricultural products are seriously affected. Even the spread of tele-communication networks is not uniform in the block. While the central region has a greater access to telecommunication facilities, the southern and northern regions are wholly deprived of this.

Power

Eventhough electricity is supplied to most requirement of the villages in the block, yet the poor households are found to be not using electricity due to poor economic condition. Besides, frequent load shedding which continues for hours together and high tariff of electricity also prevent poor households for the consumption of electricity. The Government, therefore, is to take necessary steps for reducing tariff rates which are high at present.

The electricity supply in the block, more particularly in the north and south regions, is also irregular and of low voltage. This might be due to the higher consumption of electricity than the stipulated supply. In the block, there is illegal use of electricity not only by the poor but also by the affluent. This practice need be checked. The stable supply of electricity is a precondition for industrial development. State Government needs to take effective steps in this direction.

The power position in the block can be improved by first checking the misutilisation of power. This can be done by imposing penality on the illegal user. This should be strictly adhered to by surprise checking. This will improve the supply distribution of power position in the block as the power supply will be increased to the actual consumers after the removal of illegal users.

There are also wilful defaulters. Revenue collection is lower due to these defaulters. This should be checked by cutting the supply of power to them. The household as a unit be made responsible for the misuse of power. Power supply need not be restored unless the household clears up all the past dues. This must be strictly enforced and for this inspectors and linemen of the Electricity Department need to visit the rural areas regularly and motivate the people for prompt payment. For encouraging prompt payment of electricity bills, rebates of higher amount may be allowed to consumers in rural areas compared to urban areas. This can increase the revenue collection, which can be utilised in a better manner for improving power position in the block.

Another factor that needs immediate attention for maintaining regularly in the supply of power is the removal and replacement of old and wornout transformers by new ones. It is admitted by most of the functionaries that supply of power in the panchayats is hardly regular, at best it comes for 2 to 3 hours in a day. Cottage and handicraft units operating in the block remain unutilized due to irregular supply of power. Hence, it is suggested that the old transformers be replaced by new ones. Besides, there is need for installing more transformers to cater to the needs of people in rural areas who are engaged in several productive activities. For this, the rural electricity corporation and GRIDCO need to have working cooperation and coordination to solve the problems of transmission and distribution of electricity in rural areas. As it seems, such type of co-orperation is rarely existing in the block.

Education

Education is insufficiently targeted for the benefit of the poor in the Begunia block. That's why the literacy level among the poor and particularly among the SC and ST remains much lower as compared to other castes. Improvement in literacy among the poor depends on their access to pre-primary and primary education. This also increases cognitive skills and earning potential of the poor and hungry.

The Anganwadi centres opened by the State Government in all the districts to provide pre-primary education and nutrition care are absent in the block. Therefore, it is of utmost necessity to open the Anganwadi centres in the block with immediate effect. For the participation of the poor and hungry in literacy programme steps should be taken to universalise the primary education among the poor. Though midday meal scheme is a better instrument to increase the attendance of the children of the poor families yet it has the main attraction of food, and education of these children has been side-tracked in many cases. Furthermore, the quality of food provided under the mid-day meal scheme is below minimum nutritious standard in many schools. Steps should be taken to improve the quality of food supplied through mid-day meals and to maintain the quantity as per the provision under the scheme. The poor should be provided with other facilities like free books, food and clothes. Adequate scholarship facilities among the poor should be provided to attract the poor boys and girls. Besides this, technical schools like ITI's and Polytechniques etc. be given importance in order to impart training to them. All these steps will help in increasing the literacy and skill among the poor and hungry.

Health

One of the major objectives of development is to enhance the quality of life through improvement of health and health related services for the poor in the society. In this regard, Begunia block seems to have lagged far behind the others. In order to provide the health care to the vulnerable sections, specific measures are needed to be followed.

First of all, there is dearth of doctors and nurses in the hospitals and primary health centres of the block. Several hospitals and dispensaries are manned by one doctor and one or two nurses, although the approved strength of the doctors and nurses are more. In view of this, the filling up vacant posts in the hospitals and dispensaries both at the centre and in the peripheries need be given urgent attention.

There is also irregular attendance of existing doctors and nurses. In most of the hospitals midwives are totally absent and for this the pregnant women face a lot of difficulties at the time of delivery. Many Panchayat Secretaries and Sarapanchs have confessed that the doctors are used to stay mostly in Khurda and Bhubaneswar and pay a visit to the hospitals in which they are working only once or twice in a week and that too for a short period only. Steps, therefore, should be taken to check the irregular attendance of the doctors and nurses in the hospitals and health centres. Due to their irregular attendance patients suffer a lot. Adequate medicines are not provided to the patients even in the case of common diseases. Due to this the poor suffer a lot on account of their abject poverty. There is no difference between the poor and the rich in such cases as both of them are advised to buy medicine from the open market without any support from the hospitals. If the poor can be provided with free medicines even for common diseases their health status will increase and they will work for a longer time. In case of major diseases, assistance should be provided to the poor from a charitable fund created by the Government for the purpose. In majority of cases due to lack of purchasing power the poor patients avoid treatment and suffer from many diseases.

For the development of health services, health worker at the level of sub-centres be properly trained and motivated. And mobile health units with specialists, medicines, equipment and vaccination facilities should be established so as to cater to the needs of the poor suffering from different diseases.

The Block has no Integrated Child Development Services (ICDS) centre. The objectives of this programme are; to prevent malnutrition among the most vulnerable groups and to promote health through periodic medical visits, immunisation, and health education on the use and demand of health service among low income families. This will help in increasing the health status of the children and women in the most vulnerable sections and hungry in the block. Besides this, stress need be given for the development of family planning since most of the poor families are overburdened with large number of dependent children and aged persons above sixty. On account of their maintenance of these dependant children and aged persons, the poor families are forced to spend quite a sizeable portion of their income. Consequently they fail to undertake any productive activities with scant income. Hence, in order to improve the living standard of the poor and to enable them to contribute their might for productive activities, family planning measures need be encouraged in a vigorous scale.

Drinking Water

To lead a healthy life it is necessary to provide safe drinking water to the poor. The Government has taken steps to provide safe drinking water by digging wells and installing tubewells in the Begunia block. However, the mere provision will not be sufficient if the proper follow up measures are not undertaken. A significant proportion of tubewells in the block are not functioning properly. Proper care has not been taken to improve the position by local authorities engaged for the purpose. Similarly in the open wells disinfectants are rarely used for which the poor have take impure water. Due to the lack of safe drinking water the poor are affected by several water borne diseases on many occassions. Hence, care should be taken to provide safe drinking water in all Panchayats of the Begunia block. Furthermore, the problem of drinking water is especially more acute durisng summer season. In summer season, poor rural families are found to be procuring water from distant ponds and from *'chuas'* made in the river beds. In extreme summer and drought occasions even these sources fail to meet the needs of the poor families. As a result, very often they are forced to use unsafe drinking water which leads to different diseases.

Besides the tubewells and tubewells, there are some ponds which are, though used for bathing purpose, yet they meet the drinking water requirement. Most of these ponds are not in good conditions and need to be renovated. Since the water of these ponds are usually used for bathing of animals, the water gets contaminated by several insects and becomes unsafe for drinking purposes. This can be prevented only by having more tubewells and dugwells.

III

ALLOCATION AND PRIORITISATION OF INVESTMENT IN DIFFERENT SECTORS

Proper allocation of investment in different sectors is required for plannexcd development of an economy. Moreover, it gets more important particularly when there is paucity of funds. In a poor state like Orissa, where is severe financial problem, the priority of investment in each sector also needs to be given more emphasis. Therefore, the present study has made an attempt in the following to allocate resource in different growth sectors and to make prioritisation of investment in each sector.

(a) Allocation of Investment

For the development of above growth sectors in the line of measures suggested, there is a need for effective allocation of resources. Though we have identified a number of catalysts for growth, all are not equally important and hence, do not required the equal proportion of investment. Considering the importance of different catalysts for growth the development in the block, we have presented a proposal for allocation of investment in different sectors for a period of five years. The percentage share of the proposed allocation is depicted in Table 6.1 and this is followed by a detailed note on the sectoral investment.

Agriculture being the largest sector in the Bugunia block, with a significant proprotion of population depending on it, we allocate a higher proportion of investment to this sector (Table 7.1). Since there is a meagre development of irrigation in the block, and the development of irrigation is needed in all the Gram Panchayats of the block a huge amount of investment is necessary for its development. Considering the importance of irrigation in the block, we allocate 25.65 per cent for the development of irrigation. The allocation of investment for the other agricultural development, and activities allied to agriculture comes out to be 11.0 per cent of total investment. Due to the importance of dairy and pisciculture in the block, we allocate about 4 per cent to these two sectors.

Industry is also an important economic sector, which can provide more employment in the block. But there is a meagre development of industrial sector in the block. We allocate 7.21 per cent of investment to this sector. Due to the importance of agriculture in the block, we allocate a higher percentage of investment to agro-based industries (3.91 per cent). However, village industries, like handloom, have a significant importance in the block. As such 3.3 per cent of investment is allocated for the development of these industries in the block.

Power and transport are two important features of infrastructure for economic development. For the development of agriculture and industry the development of these two sectors is of utmost necessity. Realising this, a total allocation of 6.7 per cent is made for these two sectors.

Besides the development of the above sectors, specific rural development programmes, like wage and self-employment, PDS, OAP, etc., which are targeted to the poor and hungry have great importance in the block. We, therefore, allocate about 30 per cent of investment for the rural development in the block.

However, the above allocation of investment in different sectors can benefit the poor hungry if and only if they are aware of different programmes and actively participate in these programmes. We feel that a huge investment is necessary for the physical and social development of the poor in the block. Therefore, we allocate a significantly higher proportion of investment (about 20.0 per cent) for the social development in the block. Health and education being equally important, allocation of about 10.0 per cent of investment to each sector is proposed.

(b) Prioritisation of Investment in Different Sectors

Not only the planned allocation of investment is required for economic development in the block, but the prioritisation of investment is also necessary. The suggestion for investment in different sectors in order of their priority is presented in the following.

1. Agriculture and Allied Activities

(a) Irrigation
(b) Supply of improved inputs and implements, and good variety of milch cow, better extension service.
(c) Soil and water conservation, consolidation of holding, afforesta tion, fodder cultivation etc.

2. Industry
   (a) Power
   (b) Transport and Communication
   (c) Entrepreneurship Development

3. Rural Development
   (a) Assured wage-employment
   (b) Self-employment
   (C) Public distribution system target to poor
   (d) Pension for old age, widow and disabled persons
   (e) Shelter for destitutes
   (f) Strengthening of Panchayati Raj Institutions.

4. Social Development
(A) Education
   (a) Primary and Pre-primary education
   (b) Vocational education
   (c) Adult education

(B) Health
   (a) Safe drinking water through tubewell and dugwell.
   (b) Better health care facilities.
      (i) Provision of infrastructure like dispensaries and doctors to all GPs.
      (ii) Adequate supply of medicine
      (iii) Stress for eradication of Malaria, Fileria and Leprosy.
   (c) Sanitation
      (i) Provision of Safety/Barapali latrine in all village
      (ii) Adequate drainage facilities
      (iii) Importance for spraying of disinfectants etc.

Once the prioritisation of investment is undertaken on the lines suggested above, it will help to accelerate the growth process in

Begunia block, thereby contributing significantly to help the people, now living below the poverty line, to cross the same easily and smoothly.

Table 6.1

Allocation of Investment Recommended for Different Sectors of the Block for a Period of Five Years (1998-99 to 2002-03)

Sl. No.	*Sector*	*Allocation*
1.	Agriculture and allied	7.33
a)	Agriculture & Co-operation	25.65
b)	Irrigation	
c)	Allied Activities	
i)	Dairy	1.83
ii)	Pisciculture	1.83
	Total (1)	36.64
2	Industrial Development	
	a) Agro Industry	3.91
	b) Handloom Industry	3.30
	Total(2)	7.21
3.	Power	3.03
4.	Transport	3.66
5.	Rural Development (Poverty eradication & PDS) •	29.92
6.	Social Development	
	a) Education	9.77
	b) Health & Drinking Water	9.77
	Total (6)	19.54
7.	Grand Total	100.00

•

Detailed Sectoral Investment

It is difficult to concretise the exact allocation of investment to be made for a block in a year. This is because, block level planning is not made and there is overlapping of allocation in different sectors. Furthermore, some sectors are not confined to the boundary of a block, and hence, data for the block are difficult to collect within a short span of time. There are a number of other problems relating to data for a block. Within these constraints, we present the approximate allocations of funds made in 1996-97 for different sectors for the development of Begunia block and try to forecast the probable allocation of funds required for the next five years for the rapid development of Begunia block.

It was found that during 1996-97 a sum of Rs. 398.77 lakh was allocated for the overall development of Begunia block. Of this total allocation, rural development and poverty alleviation programmes had received the highest allocation of Rs. 107.61 lakh (Table 7.2). This is followed by Public Distribution System (Rs. 100.00 lakh). Both these together had the share of more than 50 per cent of the total allocation of funds in the block. Agricultural sector, including irrigation and co-operative, received about Rs. 71.58 lakh during the year 1996-97. Within agriculture, the share of irrigation was the highest (Rs. 33.29 lakh), but it had received less than 10.0 per cent of total allocation. In the social sector, education received the highest allocation, mostly due to the higher allocation for mid-day meal scheme (about Rs. 36.10 lakh). Health and Sanitation had received an amount of Rs. 28.60 lakh during the year. Within health only medicine and equipment had an expenditure of about Rs. 4.08 lakh during the year.

It is seen that a large portion of allocation was devoted to poverty eradication programme and less importance was given to long-term growth of the economy. Therefore, there is need for reallocation of funds to different sectors and to increase funds for long-term growth of the Begunia economy. An attempt has been made here to forecast the total amounts of funds to be required for the development of the block and their reallocation in different sectors for a period of five years from 1998-99 to 2002-03

Agriculture and Cooperation

For agricultural development in the block, there is the need for making provisions for soil and water conservation, improved seeds, extension and training, and land reforms. In the year 1996-97, a total sum of Rs. 38.29 lakh was spent for these inputs in the block.

We have tried to collect data on item-wise investment of farm inputs. But, in spite of our best efforts, we could not get sufficient information. However, we could get some information from District Agricultural Office, and Soil and Water Conservation Office, Khurda. As reported by them a sum of Rs. 18.29 lakh was spent for soil and water conservation in the year 1996-97. Likewise, for improved seeds, a sum of Rs. 4.0 lakh was spent as subsidy in the block and by this about 1142 qtls of improved seeds were provided to the farmers. In the case of fertiliser, a sum of Rs. 14.0 lakh was provided as subsidy by which about 5600 qtls of fertilisers were used by the farmers. It is further reported to us that a sum of Rs. 1.0 lakh each was invested for modern implements and for extension and training. However, information about investment in pesticides and land reforms was not available to us.

In view of the investments made by the government for different agricultural inputs in the block, we propose that an investment of Rs. 1.0 crore be made for soil and water conservation for a period of five years beginning from 1998-99. Similarly, Rs. 25.0 lakh and Rs. 75.0 lakh be invested as subsidy for improved seeds and fertilisers respectively. With this amount of subsidy, the farmer would be in a position to use 3125 qtls of improved seeds and 30,000 qtls of fertilisers over a period of five years. The annual average for improved seeds and fertilisers, thus, comes to about 625 qtls and 6,000 qtls respectively. This is calculated on the basis of market price of Rs. 800.00 per qtl and Rs. 250.00 per qtl for improved seeds and fertilisers respectively, which are subject to change depending upon market conditions. For modern implements, and extension andtraining, we propose an investment of Rs. 50.0 lakh and Rs. 20.0 lakh respectively for a period of five years. In case of pesticides and land reforms, we recommend an investment of Rs. 10.0 lakh and Rs. 20.0 lakh respectively in the absence of any data of investment on these items in the past.

Since agricultural is the principal economic activity in the block and the inputs mentioned above are vital for the development of agriculture, we propose a total investment of Rs. 3.0 crore for a period of five years beginning from 1998-99. With this investment, about 40,000 MTs of paddy per annum can be produced with an area of around 15,000 hectares of land.

Irrigation

In the short-run irrigation potential in Begunia block can be created through constructing Minor Irrigation Projects (MIPs), Water Harvesting Structures (WHSs), Lift Irrigation, borewell and open wells. Irrigation potential through MIPs can be created both by renovating old irrigation projects and by creating new ones. Renovation can be made for 9 completed MIPs. 10 partly derelict MIPs and 5 completely derelict MIPs[1] in order to increase the irrigation potential in the block. This can create an additional irrigation potential of 1058 hectares. By repairing the completed MIPs irrigation potential of 549 hectares can be created with an investment of Rs. 0.70 lakh per unit. The total investment, therefore, for repairing 9 completed projects will be Rs. 6.30 lakh Similarly, by renovating 10 partly derelict MIPs, irrigation potential of 338 hectares can be created with the total investment of Rs. 11.75 lakh; and by renovating 5 completely derelict projects irrigation potential of 171 hectares can be created with an investment of Rs. 8.40 lakh. The total investment for minor irrigation projects will, therefore, be Rs. 26.45 lakh.

Besides the renovation of old projects, at least 140 new MIPs can be constructed in 9 GP[2]. For construction of new MIPs the amount required per project is Rs. 2.21 lakh. The total investment for 10 new projects will, therefore, be Rs. 22.10 lakh. This can create irrigation potential of about 590 hectares.

Considering both renovation of old projects and construction of new projects, the total allocation for creating about 1648 hectares of irrigation potential will be Rs. 48.55 lakh for a period of five years from 1998-99 to 2002-03.

Irrigation potential can also be created through constructing Water Harvesting Structures (WHSs) in the block. About 37 WHSs can be constructed in 16 GPs[3]. This can create about 1802 hectares of additional irrigation potential in the block. For the construction of these projects an allocation of about Rs. 90.95 lakh is required.

Besides the flow irrigation, additional irrigation potential can be created through lift irrigation. Seven river lifts can be installed in four GPs, viz., Haza, Siko, Kantabada and Podadiha, This can create about 141.70 hectares of irrigated area with an allocation of Rs. 10.50 lakh during the period 1998-99 to 2002-03.

Regarding ground water irrigation, there is technical problem of tapping water from the ground level. This is because, stone layers are present in the ground and aquifer between two stone layers is very small. Deep tubewell, which requires large aquifer, therefore, may not be feasible in the block. Further, there is no saline zone, showing that deep tubewell is not feasible at all in the block. However, borewell can be installed in the block as it requires small aquifer. At least 25 borewells can be installed in all the GPs in northern and central regions with an investment of about Rs. 50 lakh within a period of five years from 1998-99 to 2002-03. This can create irrigation potential of about 500 hectares.

Irrigation potential can also be created through dugwell. Since it can create a small irrigation potential of about 1 acre per unit, vegetables can be grown in the command area. Fully subsidised dugwell of about 1000 can be constructed for the poor but viable farmers in the block. It can irrigate about 400 hectares area. A sum of Rs. 2.50 crore may be allocated for dugwell for a period of five years from 1998-99.

Besides the irrigation potential in the short-run, it can also be created in the long-run in the block. For this, water from Mahanadi river can be brought to Brutanga and a medium project can be constructed there. Approximately 3000 hectares of irrigation potential can be created through this project. However, this will require a huge amount of money and a long gestation period. We suggest for allocating a total sum of Rs. 6.0 crore for a period of five years from 1998-99.

The total allocation for creation of additional irrigation potential including renovation both in the short-run and in the long-run, comes out to Rs. 10.50 crore for a period of five years from 1998-99. With this amount of investment about 7491.70 hectares of irrigation potential can be created in the block.

Dairy

In Begunia block, there is plenty of scope for promoting dairy development. As per the available statistics the block has, at present, .6055 local milch cows and 165 cross-bred cows. With this number of milch cows, milk production per day during 1996-97 was about 3.68 thousand litres. For the coming five years beginning from 1998-99, the milk production in the block can be enhanced by increasing the number of cross-brea cows. We propose that, during this five year period, the number of cross-bred cows need to be increased by 400. As per the available information, for the establishment of a diary unit, 10 cross-bred cows are necessary. Accordingly, with the additional 400 cross-bred cows, a total number of 40 dairy units will come up in the next five years in the Begunia block. These dairy units need to be set up in almost all the GPs having 2 dairy units in each GP. It is reported that, for establishing a dairy unit, a sum of Rs. 2.50 lakh is required. Accordingly, for establishing 40 dairy units, a sum of Rs. 100.0 lakh is to be invested and of these, the government has to spend only 50.0 per cent of the cost. The allocation for creating 40 dairy units, thus comes to about, Rs. 50.0 lakh for a period of five years.

In addition to the existing milk production of 3.68 thousand litres per day, there will be another 2 thousand litres per day on account of the increase in the number of cross-bred cows by 400. The total milk production thus comes to about 5.68 thousand litres per day. On the basis of this milk production, there is the possibility of having two chilling plants; each having the capacity of 2000 LPD. This can be set up in Haza and Begunia respectively*. Presently, there is one chilling plant at Tangi, which is situated at a short distance from the Begunia block. But it is not working properly and does not run upto the full capacity. Since the two chilling plants, as recommended by us may not be established immediately, they can be established in

* As per the information received from Sub-Divisional Veterinary Office, Khurda.

a phased manner; first beginning with the Haza within a period of five years and the second one can be taken up in the next five years period after looking into the performance of the first chillling plant. For establishing one chilling plant, the total cost comes to about Rs. 15.0 lakh and this amount needs to be invested by the government to start with.

Besides the production and preservation of milk, veterinary services should also be strengthened by supplying adequate medicines, surgical equipments and others. Although the actual amount of investment for veterinary medicines and surgical equipments are not available at the block and the district level, yet we got the information from the sub-divisional veterinary office that approximately Rs. 60.0 thousand was spent for veterinary medicines and equipments in 1996-97. Accordingly, we suggest for an investment of Rs. 5.0 lakh for a period of five years for medicines and surgical equipments to increase the yield of mild and provide veterinary services for more animals.

There was no investment for fodder cultivation in 1996-97. But looking into the importance of fodder cultivation for dairy development, we suggest an investment of Rs. 5.0 lakh for a period of five years. With this amount of investment, fodder cultivation can be started in panchayats like Haza, Begunia and Sarua with the active participation of the people.

In view of the suggestions made above, a total sum of Rs. 10.0 lakh would be invested in the next five years for veterinary medicines, surgical; equipments and fodder cultivation.

For the dairy development comprising establishment of 40 dairy units, one chilling plant, purchase of medicines, surgical instruments, creation of fodder cultivation and extension and training facilities, a total sum of Rs. 75.0 lakh will be invested for a period of five years beginning from 1998-99.

Pisciculture

Begunia block has 166.13 ha of water area, Out of this water area, 138 pisciculture units are developed in 50.53 ha. The total fish production from these pisciculture units is reported to be 150 metric tonnes (1500 qtls) per annum in the year 1996-97**.

For the next five years, we propose to increase fish production by developing more water area for pisciculture. In order to achieve this, we recommend for developing another 30 hectares of water area for pisciculture units. We find that, with the increase in the additional 30 ha of water area, about 80 pisciculture units can be established over a period of five years. With the establishment of additional 80 pisciculture units, the total fish production will increase by 100 metric tonnes (1000 qtl) per annum, and it will generate direct employment of at least 160 persons in the block.

The additional pisciculture units, that we envisage for coming five years, can be established in Panchayats like Sarua and Baghamari in central Begunia; Podadiha, Simor and Badaberana in northern Begunia; and Haza, Siko and Deuli in Southern Begunia, where favourable conditions for the development of pisciculture are available.

As per the estimate given by District Fishery Department, a sum of Rs. 0.63 lakh is required for establishing one pisciculture unit comprising working capital, block capital and expenses of marketing. For establishing additional 80 pisciculture units, as suggested by us, a total sum of Rs. 50.0 lakh will be invested over a period of five years, which the State Government has to undertake for the development of the fishery sector in the block. The increased fish production has a wide prospect for marketing in places like Banki, Bolagarh, Nayagarh, Khurda and the distant places like Bhubaneswar.

Fish production can also be increase by developing and renovating old tanks and ponds used for pisciculture. In order to promote them there is the need for excavating the ponds and tanks, supplying of fish-breeds, replacing of old nets and equipments by newer ones and offering training and guidance to the fishermen. For all these, we propose an investment of Rs. 25.0 lakh to be undertaken by the State Government for a period of five years beginning from 1998-99.

** As per the data supplied by the District Fishery Officer, Khurda.

For the improvement of pisciculture, which includes establishment of additional pisciculture units, establishment and renovation of old ponds and tanks and bringing new lease of life to the existing ponds, we recommend for an allocation of Rs. 75.0 lakh for a period of five years.

Agro-Industries

Begunia block provides scope for the establishment of agro-industries like cashew-processing units, food processing units and cold storages.

As per the available information received from Soil and Water Conservation Department of Khurda district, cashew plantation covers an area of 3092 acres (1250 ha). The production in the year 1996-97, from these cashew plantations, was 1190 qtls. It appears that the production of cashew nuts is quite encouraging in the block. In view of this, we recommend that more efforts need to be made towards creating more cashew plantations in the block. For this, we recommend to set up cashew plantations in an additional area of 3000 acres (i.e., 1215 ha) within a period of five years. Since an acre of cashew plantation consisting of 100 plants costs about Rs. 100.00, the total amount required for promoting cashew plantation in additional 3000 acres (i.e., 1215 ha) will be around Rs. 30.0 lakh. As a result of this, 3 lakh additional cashew plants can be created in the block by which the quantity of cashew production will be quite substantial.

Since the existing cashew plantations are mostly located in Panchayats like Kunjuri, Routpada and Botalma, these GPs need to be further strengthened. The additional cashew plantations, as proposed by us, for covering an area of 3000 acres may be established in Durgapur, Govindpur, Radhakantapur, Begunia and Sarua.

With the present production of cashew nuts, i.e., 1192 qtls, when the prospective production of cashew nuts are added after the creation of additional cashew plantations in 3000 acres over a period of five years, the total production of cashew nuts will be about 2300 qtls. With this production, a number of cashew processing units can be set up in Begunia block.

Presently, there is a cashew processing unit in Daltola village of Kunjuri GP. But this is not sufficient and adequate to generate more income and employment. We, therefore, recommend for the setting up of an another cashew processing unit in central region, preferably in Begunia GP. The cost for setting up of an additional unit of cashew processing industry, on the basis of prevailing market price, will be around Rs.70.0 lakh Hence, this amount need be invested in the block during the next five year period by the government.

Next to cashew processing units, there is also a demand for rice mills in Begunia block. We, therefore, recommend three paddy processing mills at a total cost of Rs. 10.0 lakh in Haza, Beghamari and Badaberana, the major rice producing areas of the block.

In Begunia, there is also a large scope for the production of vegetables. The available data reveal that the total production of vegetables in the year 1996-97 was 9227.53 MTs from 2176 ha covered under vegetables. We propose that the area under vegetables in the coming five years will increase to about 3500 ha giving rise to a total production of 15,000 MTs of vegetables. With this, 4 food processing units like Chilli Sauce, pickle, etc. can be set up in the block covering the Panchayats like Haza, Baghamari, Pongarsingh and Simor. In view of the importance of food processing units in Begunia blocks, we propose to invest a sum of Rs.10.0 lakh over a period of five years for the development of these industries.

The demand for a cold storage by the farmers was largely felt by us at the time of field study. Cold storage facility is essential for preserving surplus vegetables for a longer duration. And this is also advantageous for the food processing units. We, therefore, propose that a cold storage unit may be set up in Begunia GP at a cost of Rs. 40.0 lakh for the benefit of the farmers.

In view of the above observations, a total sum of Rs. 160.0 lakh may be invested over a period of five years for activities like development of cashew plantations, establishments of cashew processing units, establishment of food processing units, paddy processing (rice) mills and cold storage.

Handloom Industry

There is potential for the development of handloom industry in Begunia block. As per the data supplied by the Assistant Director of Textiles, Khurda division, there are, at present, 1029 handlooms in the block and about 2955 persons are employed in these industries. It is observed that no powerloom is in operation at present in the block. There are a total number of 11 co-operative societies which are mainly undertaking marketing of handloom products. Besides, they also supply the raw materials to the weavers for their use in individual units. It is also important that a sum of Rs. 5.46 lakh was spent by goverment through co-operative societies during the year 1996-97 under the project package scheme.

In view of this, we like to recommend for setting up of 20 handloom co-operative units and 6 powerloom co-operative units in the next five years beginning from 1989-99. It is to be noted that such co-operative units did not exist earlier in the block. We have further come to know that a co-operative unit of handloom consists of 5 looms and a powerloom consists of 6 looms. For establishing one handloom co-operative unit and a powerloom co-operative unit, sums of Rs. 1.5 lakh and Rs. 5.0 lakh respectively are required. On the basis of this unit cost, a total amount of Rs. 60.0 lakh is ear-marked for investment in the handloom and powerloom sectors of the block. Since southern Begunia provides ample opportunities for the development of handloom industries, we intend to recommend these co-operative handloom & powerloom units to be set up in places like, Routpada, Dingar, Botllma and Siko.

Taking into consideration of the number of handloom and powerloom co-operative units that will come up during the next five years, we further recommend for the setting up of a small scale textile unit at a cost of Rs. 15.0 lakh to be invested by the government in the Routpada GP of Begunia block.

The modernisation and renovation of existing handloom units in the block are not adequately met. We, therefore, propose a sum of Rs. 40.0 lakh to be invested by the government for the modernisation and renovation of the existing handloom units, including the newer ones for a period of five years.

The training of the weavers should also receive priority in the block. In order to acquaint the weavers to new designs latest technology, and improved tool and implements, training and guidance are necessary. For this, we recommend a sum of Rs. 20.0 lakh to be invested by the government over a period of five years for imparting up-to-data training and guidance to the weavers working in the existing units, and those who will be asked to handle the new units.

For all the above programmes, we propose a total amount of Rs. 135.0 lakh to be invested over a period of five years beginning from 1998-99.

Road & Transport

The road and transport facilities in the block are not developed. There are some villages in Botalma & Durgapur GPs which are not connected by any type of road. We, therefore, recommend that at leas 10 kms of *kutcha* road be constructed in the coming five years in these panchayats. Similarly, the connecting roads between one GP and the other are found to be *kutcha* at present. Such types of kutcha roads are mostly seen between Sagadabhanga and Siko GP, Begunia and Badaberana, Begunia and Kasntabada. We propose that at least 20 kms of pucca road be constructed over a period of 5 years.

It is reported that for constructing 1 km of *kutcha* road a sum of Rs. 1.5 lakh is required. Similarly, for constructing 1 km of *pucca* road a sum of Rs. 6.0 lakh is needed. Accordingly, the recommended amount of investment to be undertaken for a period of five years by the government comes to about Rs. 15.0 lakh & Rs. 120.0 lakh respectively. This together becomes rs. 135.0 lakh for the period of five years.

It is noticed during the field study that the block did not have adequate number of buses plying between the block headquarters and the interior panchayats. Since government buses are inoperative, one private bus is found to be running casually between Begunia block and distantly located panchayats like Deuli and Sikko. We, therefore, propose an investment of Rs. 15.0 lakh for the purchase of two buses for improvement of transport facility in the block.

Accordingly, for the purpose of construction of roads and purchase of buses a total sum of Rs. 150.0 lakh is to be invested over a period of five years.

Power

The distribution of eiectricity is not satisfactory in Begunia block. Whatever distribution is there, it is concentrated more in the central region of Begunia block. The distribution of electricity in northern and southern regions is irregular and erratic. This is due to old and worn out transformers of low capacity. In spite of our enquiry, we could not get the data regarding the number of existing transformer and the number of old and worn out transformers in different parts of Begunia block. Even we failed to obtain data regarding the capacity of the trans formers set up in Begunia block. However, we could get the information that a total sum of Rs. 10.0 lakh was spent in power sector in Begunia block in 1996-97.

We feel that there is a need for replacing the old and worn out transformers by new ones. In this connection we recommend that additional 20 transformers having the capacity of 63 KV and 10 transformers having the capacity of 100 KV may be installed in the next five years in different regions of the block for regular and uninterrupted supply of electricity. It is reported that a 63 KV transformer costs around Rs, 40,000.00 and a 100 KV transformer costs about Rs. 60,000.00. The total amount for installing additional 30 transformers thus comes to about Rs. 14.0 lakh, which is to be invested for a period of five years in Begunia block.

Apart from the cost of the transformers to be incurred by the government, a sum of Rs. 60.0 lakh is to be invested for the installation of the transformers which includes barbed wire, poles, high conductive wires, etc. in different localities.

The government has, further, the obligation to distribute electricity free of cost in favour of the weaker sections, who are below the poverty line. For this, an amount of Rs. 50.0 lakh is recommended for five years for the purpose of investment by the government.

In view of the above measures recommended by us, a sum of

Rs. 124.0 lakh is to be invested in the power sector over a period of five years in Begunia block.

Education

It is observed from the field study that the literacy performance of Begunia block is satisfactory. But in cases of SC & ST, the literacy performance appears to be discouraging. In order to bring them to the mainstream of education we recommend for the adoption of universal primary education throughout the block. As reported by School Inspector, Begunia, the number of existing primary schools in Begunia block is 98. But these primary schools have failed to cover all the children of SC & ST categories. We, therefore, propose to increase additional number of 15 primary schools in order to cover all the SC & ST children under primary education. These additional schools have to be set up in villages coming under southern and northern regions of Begunia block. As reported to us, the cost of constructing a primary school having two rooms with drinking water and toilet facilities costs around Rs. 2.0 lakh. On the basis of the cost per primary school, we propose an investment of Rs. 30.0 lakh in Begunia block over a period of five years.

The need for adult education also deserves or attention. Presently, there are 52 adult education centres in Begunia block. Looking at the number of old and aged persons we recommend an additional number of 20 adult education centres in the block. As reported to us, for one adult education centre the government spends about Rs 20.0 thousand per annum. Accordingly, a sum of Rs. 20.0 lack is to be invested for the establishment of 20 adult education centres over a period of five years. This amount covers distribution of books, salary of teachers, class-room accessories, etc. These adult education centres are again to be given priority of opening in villages belonging to southern and northern regions.

At present there is no technical institution worth the name of I.T.I in Begunia block. Taking into consideration the demand of the people for technical education, we recommend for the establishment of a mini I.T.I. in Begunia GP. Likewise, we also feel to recommend a vocational training institute preferably to be set up in

Kunjuri GP. For these two training institutes, we recommend an investment of Rs. 70.0 lakh and Rs. 30.0 lakh respectively over a period of five years beginning from 1998-99.

In order to encourage the attendance among the children of BPL females, the government has introduced mid-day meal programme during the 8th Five Year Plan. In the year 1996-97, the mid-day meal programme had covered 14863 children in the block. In the said year, a sum of Rs. 36.0 lakh was spent for the programme.

It is observed that the cost of mid-day meal per day per child was Rs. 1.0. This appears to be insufficient. We, therefore, strongly feel that the cost per meals per child be enhanced to at least Rs. 1.40. The mid-day meal programme covers a number of items like purchase of items, fuel, utensils and remuneration of the cook and the helper.

In order to cover 200 additional children each year over and above the existing number of children covered by the programme, at present, i.e., 14863, we propose an investment of Rs. 50.0 lakh per annum, totalling Rs. 2.50 crore over a period of five years.

In view of the measures adopted for expansion of eduction in Begunia block, a total sum of Rs. 4.0 crore is to be spent in the next five years.

Health

Development of health infrastructure has received top priority in the block. As reported from the office of the Medical Officer, Botalma, there were one Community Health Centre, 10 Primary Health Centres (PHCs) and 19 Dispensaries in the block in the year 1995-96. The valuable information indicates that the block is well served by medical institutions. We, therefore, do not propose any additional PHC/dispensaries in the coming five years for the block. We have come to know that the block has a Homeopathy dispensary in Kunjuri GP. We propose an Ayurvedic hospital to be set up in Begunia to meet the demand of the people. For the construction of an Ayurvedic hospital, a sum of Rs. 10.0 lakh may be invested.

We have marked deficiencies in the various components necessary for running the PHCs and dispensaries. The available data indicate that there were only 24 beds in the hospitals of the block. This appears to be insufficiently. We, therefore, propose that each dispensary and PHC should have two beds; one for male and the other for female. Similarly, the number of beds in CHC, Botalma needs to be increased to 16. Thus, there is need for having additional 540 beds over and above the existing 24 beds as on 1995-96 in the block over a period of five years. For this, we propose to allocate a sum of Rs. 1.0 lakh.

Medicines from the hospitals are mostly available for common diseases. For chronic diseases the patients are asked to procure such medicines from the open market. It is reported by the medical authorities that a sum of Rs. 4.08 lakh was spent for medicines and medical instruments in the years 1996-97. This amount appears to be inadequate. Taking into consideration the number of patients attending hospitals per day, we purpose that a sum of Rs. 49.0 lakh is to be invested for medicines and medical equipments by the government over a period of five years.

As mentioned earlier, there were 30 health centres comprising CHC, PHC and dispensaries in the block during 1995-96. However, we could notice that the number of doctors working in such centres accounted for only 13, which appears to be too small. We, therefore, recommend that each of the PHCs and dispensaries must have at least one doctor. But in CHC, we recommend the number of doctors needs to be 5 including the specialists, particularly in the field of Gynaecology and E.N.T. Besides, we recommend that the health department should ensure that the doctors appointed attend to their duties. It is very often complained that the doctors appointed remain very often absent in the Centres. For all these, we propose to recommend an investment of Rs. 100.0 lakh over a period of five years. Apart from salary, this will also cover the cost of construction of the quarters for the doctors.

We came to know during the course of our field study that there were only 26 nurses and mid-wives spread over 30 hospitals operating in the block. This number appears to be grossly inadequate. We, therefore, recommend that the number of Mid-wives and nurses should be increased by at least 20 over and above the present number of 26.

We noticed that all the hospitals did not have pharmacists. Only in some hospitals like Begunia, Podadiha, Govindapur, etc. we could come across pharmacists working in the dispensaries. As reported to us, there were only 16 pharmacists working in 30 hospitals of Begunia block. We, therefore, propose that each of the PHCs and dispensaries should have at least one pharmacist. And for CHC, we propose that a total number of three pharmacists be appointed.

In course of our discussion with the medical officer, Botalma, we were reported that the block has no ambulance. In order to provide ambulance facilities we propose 2 ambulances for the block. For this, it is suggested to invest a sum of Rs. 15.0 lakh in the block.

The block did not implement ICDS programme in the past. But ICDS and Anganwadi are essential from the point of view of eradicating hunger and poverty. This programme is useful to solve the problem of malnutrition and undernutrition. Accordingly, we propose that the ICDS centre be located in the block headquarters, while 20 Anganwadi centres be distributed in all GPs to start with. For this programme, we earmark a sum of Rs. 1.0 crore to be invested over a period of five years. The block has a number of leprosy patients. During our field study we could notice such patients in the Hirapur village of Botalma GP. Such leprosy patients are more or less visible in other GPs also. Presently there are no leprosy eradication centres in the block. As a result of this, the leprosy patients face a lot of difficulties. We, threfore, propose that in the next five years a leprosy eradication centre may be set up in the Botalma GP. The rehabilitation of lepers also received our attention. For all this, we propose an investment of Rs. 30.0 lakh for the leprosy eradication centre and Rs. 50.0 lakh for the rehabilitation of the lepers, thus making the total of Rs. 80.0 lakh.

For all the above programmes, the likely amount of investment will be Rs. 3.55 crore in the next five years.

Drinking Water

Drinking water, at present, is mostly supplied through tubewells installed in the block. As per the data received from the office of Rural Water Supply and Sanitation, there were about 511 functioning tubewells and 77 non-functioning tubewells during 1996-97. This shows that the block had a total number of 588 tubewells compresing both functioning and non-functioning tubewells.

In the coming five years, we propose that the number of tubewells be increased to 611. That is, an additional number of 100 functioning tubewells. Out of this 100 additional tubewells, 23 tubewells will be newly installed and 77 tubewells will replace the defunct tubewells. For this, we recommend a sum of Rs. 40.0 lakh over a period of five years. This cost is calculated on the lossing the cost of a tubewell at market price of Rs. 40,000.00. The additional 23 new tubewells are to be installed in Sarua, Badaberana and Govindpur GPs.

Apart from the tubewells, there were also 496 open wells in the block. It is reported to us that in two-thirds of the open wells, the water has become polluted due to the absence of the use of any disinfectants. In order to have adequate safe drinking water, we propose a sum of Rs. 5.0 lakh for the use of disinfectants.

Accordingly, in the next five years, we recommend a sum of Rs. 45.0 lakh for the creation of additional tubewells, renovation of existing wells and the use of disinfectants.

Rural Development

For rural development mainly two programmes are in operation in the block. They are: Self-Employment Programme and Wage Employment Programme. In Self-Employment Programme, we have IRDP, DWCRA, TRYSEM, etc. For wage employment, we have JRY & EAS. Under Self employment Programme, activities like dairy, goattery, sheepery, petty business, etc. are undertaken. They are undertaken through schemes like IRDP & DWCRA. On the other hand, TRYSEM covers activities like tailoring, cycle repairing, carpentry, etc. and imparts training to the persons below the poverty line who are expected to undertake these activities.

It is reported to us that, in the year 1996-97, a sum of Rs. 40.0 lakh was spent in self-employment programmes covering IRDP,

DWCRA, etc. It is further reported that a total number of 800 families received benefit under this programme. In view of the importance of self-employment in Begunia block, we propose an investment of Rs. 2.50 crore over a period of five years beginning from 1998-99. With this investment, it is presumed that a total number of 4150 families living below the poverty line will get the opportunity of self-employment during the five year period.

As mentioned earlier there is greater scope for wage-employment in Begunia block. In the year 1996-97, sum of Rs. 60.0 lakh was spent for the programme like JRY and EAS. With this investment a total number of 144 thousand employment was generated in Begunia block. In view of the success of wage-employment, we recommend an investment of Rs. 3.5 crore over a period of five years, which would generate employment to the extent of 835 thousand, and increase of six fold of employment over the years 1996-97.

For both self-employment and wage-employment, therefore, we recommend a total sum of Rs. 6.0 crore to be invested over a period of five years in Begunia block.

Under rural development, housing for the homeless needs utmost attention. Houses to these homeless persons are usually provided through Indira Awas Yojana (IAY). The beneficiaries covered are SC, ST and bonded labourers. As reported by DRDA, Khurda a sum of Rs. 19.40 lakh was invested under IAY programme in Begunia block in the year 1996-97. With this investment 121 houses were constructed with unit cost of Rs. 16.0 thousand per house. In spite of this investment and number of houses constructed, we have noticed that the bonded labourers and a majority of the STs have not got the benefit. The scheme has benefited mostly the SC communities. With a view to cover all types of beneficiaries by providing houses we recommend an investment of about Rs. 1.0 crore over a period of five years. By this investment a total number of 606 houses will be constructed assuming the unit cost of constructing per house Rs. 16.5 thousand due to cost escalation.

Old age pension and widow pension also form an important component of rural development and poverty eradication. normally Rs.

100/- per month is given as maintenance allowance to aged persons above 60 years and widows. In the absence of any data regarding the number of pensioners benefiting from the scheme and the amount of investment undertaken by the government for the purpose, it is difficult to mention exact amount of investment of this head. However, looking into the number of old age and widow pensioners and their expectations from the government for social security, we recommend an investment of Rs. 25.0 lakh for a period of five years.

For the hungry people, food security is highly essential. This is usually undertaken by the government through Public Distribution System (PDS). Presently, rice, kerosene and sugar are provided through PDS to all the families in the block. As a result of this, the non-poor get more advantage than the poor. Even, whatever is available, the poor are also unable to buy due to low level of income.

With our emphasis on rural development, there may be more generation of employment activities in the rural areas creating more income. Under this circumstance, PDS needs to be given special attention. We, thrrefore, propose that, apart from providing rice, kerosene and sugar, the PDS must undertake to supply dhoti and saree, baby food edible oils and salt. We also recommend that the present quota of rice and kerosene per card holder be increased to 15 kgs and 5 lts respectively. Moreover, the modified PDS system should be exclusively meant for the persons living below the poverty line and the non-poor in the block should be éxcluded from the PDS. In view of all these, we recommend a sum of Rs. 5.0 crore to be invested for a period of five years in Begunia block.

The actions taken on the line suggested by us will cost an investment of Rs. 12.25 crore for poverty eradication and PDS for a period of five years.

The sector-wise allocation of funds for the block during the five years from 1998-99 to 2002-03 is presented in Table 6.3.

Table 6.2

Allocation of Funds Among Different Sectors of Begunia Block during 1996-97

(Rs.in Lakh)

Sl. No.	*Sectors*	*Allocation*
1.	Agriculture and Allied	38.29
a)	Agriculture & Co-operation	33.29
b)	Irrigation	
c)	Allied Activities	
i)	Dairy	Nil
ii)	Pisciculture	Nil
	Total(1)	71.58
2.	Industrial Development	
a)	Handloom	5.46
b)	Cashew Plantation	4.52
	Total (2)	9.98
3.	Power	10.00
4.	Transport	20.00
5.	Rural Development (Poverty eradication & PDS)	
a)	PDS	100.00
B)	Others	107.61
	Total(5)	
6.	Social Development	
a)	Education	51.00
b)	Health & Drinking Water	28.60
	Total (6)	79.60
7.	Grand Total	398.77

N.B. For some department data were not readily available. We have given a rough estimation of investment on the basis of the discussion with the functio-aries. This is only for a small number of cases.

Table 6.3

Allocation of Funds Recommended for Different Sectors of the Block for the Five Years from 1998-99 to 2002-03

(Rs. ion crore)

Sl. No.	Section	98-99	99-00	00-01	01-02	02-03	Total Five Years
1	2	3	4	5	6	7	8
1.	Agriculture and Allied						
	a) Agriculture & Co-operation	0.49	0.54	0.59	0.65	0.73	3.00
	b) Irrigation	1.72	1.89	2.08`	2.29	2.52	10.50
	c) Allied Activities`						
	i) Dairy	0.12	0.14	0.15	0.16	0.18	0.75
	ii) Pisciculture.	0.12	0.14	0.15	0.16	0.18	0.75
	Total(1)	2.45	2.71	2.97	3.26	3.61	15.00
2.	Industrial Development						
	a) Agro Industry	0.26	0.29	0.32	0.35	0.38	1.60
	b) Handloom Industry	0.22	0.24	0.27	0.29	0.33	1.35
	Total (2)	0.48	0.53	0.59	0.64	0.71	2.95
3.	Power	0.20	0.22	0.25	0.27	0.30	1.24
4.	Transport	0.24	0.28	0.30	0.32	0.36	1.50
5.	Rural Development (Poverty eradication and PDS)	2.01	2.21	2.43	2.67	2.93	12.25
6.	Social Development						
	a) Education	0.66	0.72	0.79	0.87	0.96	400
	b) Health & Drinking Water	0.66	0.72	0.79	0.87	0.96	4.00
	Total (6)	1.32	1.44	1.58	1.74	1.92	8.00
7.	Grand Total	6.70	7.39	8.12	8.90	9.83	40.94

NOTES

1 Completed MIPs are situated in 5 GPs, viz., Begunia, Sarua,Baghamari, Simor and Botalma. Partly derelict projects are found in 9 GPs, viz., Badaberana, Baghamari, Botalma, Siko, Simor, Kantabada, Pongersingh and Durgapur. Completely derelict projects are situated in 4 GPs, viz., Durgapur, Deulim Kunjuri and Podadiha.

2. The GPs are Radhakantapur, Sarua, Kantabada, Begunia, Botalma, Podadiha, Durgapur, Simor & Kunjuri.

3. The GPs are Siko, Sagadabhanga, Pongarsingh, Simor, Baghamari, Kantabada, Podadiha, Gadamanitri, Radhakantapur, Begunia, Botalma, Badaberana, Routpada, Haza, Deuli and Kunjuri.

REFERENCES

1. K.M. Mishra, *Irrigation and Economic Development,* Ashish Publishing House, New Delhi, 1990.
2. Operation Research (ORG), *Socio-Economic Appraisal of Minor Irrigation Projects__A Pilot Study in Dhenkanal District Bhubaneswar*, 1984
3. T.Satapathy, *Irrigation and Economic Development*, Ashish Publishing House, New Delhi, 1984.
4 Water and Land Management Institute (WALMI), *Report on Socio-Economic Bench Mark Survey in Action Research Area of Kuanria Medium Irrigation Project, Orissa*, Bhubaneswar, 1988.
5. R.M.Mallik, S.P Padhi and S.Meher, *Irrigation Systems in Orissa: Its Impact on Agricultural Development*, Interim Report (Submitted to ICAR), NKC Centre for Development Studies, Bhubaneswar, 1994.
6. V.Venkaiah, *Impact of Agro-Based Industries on Rural Economy,* Himalaya Publishing House, Bombay, 1987.
7. S.K.Gupta, *Development of Agro-Industries: Problems and Prospects,* Deep and Deep Publications, New Delhi, 1993.
8. Government of Orissa, *Economic Survey*: 1994-95, Directorate of Eco nomics and Statistics, Bhubaneswar, 1995.
9. R.K. Meher, *Problems and Prospects of Handloom Industries in Orissa,* NKC Centre for Development Studies, Bhubaneshwar, 1992.
10. Government of Orissa, *op.cit.*
11. Ismail Serageldin and Pirre Landell-Mills (eds) *Overcoming Global Hunger,* World Bank, 1994.
12. Kaushik Basu, Elimination of Endemic Poverty in South Asia: Some Policy Options', in J.Dreze, A.Sen and A.Hussain (eds), The *Political Economy of Hunger*, Oxford University Press, New Yourk, 1995.

13. I. Serageldin and P. Landell-Mills, *op.cit.*
14. Kaushik Basu, *op.cit,*
15. I. Serageldin and P. Landell-Mills, *op.cit.*
16. Baidyanath Misra, *Economic Profile of India,* APH Publishing Corporation, New Delhi, 1997.
17. H.S. Shylendra, 'Institutional Reform and Rural Poor: A Studyon the Distributional Performance of a Regional Rural Bank, *India Journal of Agricultural Economics,* Vol.51, No.3, July-Sept.1996.
18. H.P.Binswanger and P. Landell-Mills, *The World Banks Strategy for Reducing Poverty and Hunger,* World Bank, 1995 p. 42.
19. Kaushik Basu, *op.cit.*
20. H..P. Binswanger and P. Landell-Mills, *op.cit.*
21. I. Serageldin and P.Landell-Mills, *op.cit.*

7

Problems and Policy Prescriptions

In the foregoing analysis it has been observed that the State Government has implemented a number of programmes to undertake direct action against poverty in the Begunia Block. But the programmes have not yielded significant results. Since poverty is the root cause of hunger, the ineffectiveness of direct public action programmes to reduce poverty is a threat to the endemic hunger and undernourishment. This raises an important question, whether the direct public action programme should be continued in order to make the freedom from hunger a success?

However, it should be kept in mind that though there is a positive role of direct public action in long-term alleviation of hunger and poverty, short-term alleviation measures cannot be termined forthwith. Long-term development programmes have a long gestation period. And in the long-run, all the poor without short-term assistance may not survive. This implies that while implementing some of the long-term developmental programmes, we will have to continue some short-term remedial measures to assist the poor who go without food. However, the critical gaps and missing links identified both in implementation as well as in strategy of different programmes make the goal unrealisable. It is, therefore, necessary to correct these problems on a priority basis.

The most important problrm that needs immediate correction is the manner in which the BPL (Below Poverty Line) list is prepared. It is necessary that a full scale statistical survey of income and assets of households must be conducted in the block before the preparation of the BPL list. For this the households need be ranked with reference to a composite index of landholding and income. After this the list needs to be placed in the Gram Sabha (village meeting) for approval prior to the selection of the beneficiaries. Though in the existing system Gram Sabhas have to play a mojor role in the selection of beneficiaries, yet they are not given sufficient importance at the block level. Therefore, appropriate steps need be taken by the Government to involve Gram Sabhas in the selection of beneficiaries at the village level. The selected list there after may be displayed in the public places i.e., in the block office or in educational institutions in order to ensure correctness in the selection of beneficiaries and to plug loopholes, if any in the matter of selection.

After the selection of beneficiaries steps be taken to help the poor to received the benefits provided by the government under various poverty alleviation programmes in the rural areas. Here the role of effective implementation is very important. For successful implementation of direct public action programmes three things are necessary; (i) an efficient and clean administration, (ii) public awareness, and (iii) social activism and commitment. It is, therefore, necessary that administrative system should be efficient and incorruptible. This is a difficult problem. However, this can be done to some extent if people are made aware of the programmes launched by the government. And such awareness among the poor can be created only through education, motivation and social action. Even though direct action programmes take the form of economic measures yet their success depends upon social activism and commitment. The political constraints often make the programmes ineffective and non-functional. Hence, the participation of local leaders and NGOs with a commitment to serve and guide the poor is necessary.

One may, thus, suggest various measures for the success of direct public action programmes. However, one wonders how far such measures could be devide and adopted under the present socio-economic conditions prevailing in the block. Even if appropriate measures are devised and implemented for the benefit of hungry people, yet the question arises: are all the different programmes successful in generating additional income and employment for eliminating hunger? Which of the existing income generating programmes ought to receive priority? In order to meet these queries let us compare between self-employment and wage employment programmes adopted in the block.

It is a fact that the basic cause of hunger and poverty in rural areas is underemployment and unemployment. While adopting self-employment programmes it is assumed that the persons living below the poverty line do not have adequate access to capital assets. Therefore, self-employment programmes are intended to provide capital assets to the poor in rural areas. It is assumed that provision of such assets to the poor would help them to generate self-employment opportunities and additional income for their families. This would go a long way in reducing poverty and hunger in the rural areas. However, the self-employment programmes expect too much in terms of entrepreneurial ability on the part of the poorest of the poor, who neither have the capacity nor the aptitude to undertake self-employment activities. The provision of capital assets to such persons may not help to generate adequate self-employment in rural areas.

The poor area, however, not a homogenous group. The above model of poverty alleviation may be suitable for 'middle' or 'upper' poor households, in which members have adequate entrepreneurial ability. But it is inappropriate in the case of poorest households, where there is high degree of income insecurity. Accordingly, these households need protectional services, in the absence of which chronic poverty and hunger may persist.

As a matter of fact, wage-employment is found to be more suitable in the case of these households. This programme does not require any entrepreneurial ability. Since they are unskilled workers, manual labour can be provided by them in programmes concerned with wage labour. This will help them to earn additional income that will help to remove hunger. It is seen that employment programmes like Jawahar Rojagar Yojana (JRY) and Employment Assurance Scheme (EAS) are in vogure in Begunia block for some time. But the implementation of these programmes lack proper planning and guidance in providing assured employnment to the beneficiaries and to cover all the poorest of the poor households in the block who are able to work. These programmes, however, contain essential aspect of providing assured employment to the needy poor persons. For this a clearcut programme of providing employment of at least 100 mandays in the agricultural lean season to each poor family or to provide 300 mandays during a year would be a desirable policy in the direction of reducing hunger and poverty. According to Dandekar, while the possibilities of creating self-employment should be explored the main reliance will have to be on offering wage employment. He points out that this does not mean a perennial dependence because the 'more thrifty' provident, and enterprising' among the beneficiaries of an employment scheme are like to 'set themselves up' in the long-run and become independent[1].

However, there is no justification of implementing a number of wage-employment programmes like JRY, EAS, etc. It will only create confusion and add additional burden to the implementing authorities. A single wage-employment programme can be sufficient to achieve the goal than a multiple number of wage-employment programmes. Therefore, the different wage-employment programmes which are at present in vogure in Begunia block should be merged into one, and steps should be taken to provide assured employment in actual sense. It is, threfore, required that a clear-cut announcement regarding how assured employment can be provided to the hungry and poor should be made at the begnning of the financial year. This should include the number of projects to be handled, number of poor to be covered, number of mandays to be created, persons to be entrusted with the responsibility of undertaking the work, etc. All these should be well planned and aimed at covering all the hungry and needy poor in the block.

We have made it clear from the very beginning that poverty and hunger are not synonymous. The solution to hunger would, therefore, lie first in identifying the real hungry and then to provide them with income. The wage-employment programme does not cover all the hungry family. This is because the chronically ill, the aged, the crippled and the orphaned are unable to work in wage-employment and hence, are generally excluded from the programme.As such, the reduction of hunger through policies that encourage income and employment are not enough. They should be accompanied by food supplementation and health care in order to lead a healthy and active life.

Food supplementation to the hungry can be done either through rationed food subsidy or through nutrition monitoring programme. If the food subsidisation be choosen, it should be targeted only for the benefit of the poor through Public Distribution System (PDS). The present system of PDS which is targeted to both poor and non-poor should be abandoned and in its place only poor should be targeted. However, the PDS should cover all the necessary commodities required by the poor like millets, coarse grains etc. The quota should be made adequate. Since the poorest of the poor, particularly hungry, lack purchasing power the commodities provided to them through the PDS should be highly subsidised. In order to improve physical access of the poor, the number of fair price shops should also be increased. Likewise, in the selection of dealers to man the fairprice shops, persons with high sense of community service and commitment be selected. Black marketiers, unscrupulous persons need not be entrusted with the responsibility of distributing rationed commodities. The present PDS has failed to serve the poor people in the rural areas because many unscrupulous traders are entrusted with the responsibility of distributing commodities to the rural poor. The dealers have consolidated their financial position more at the cost of poor beneficiaries for whom the scheme is exclusively meant.

However, though food subsidisation takes care of food security it lacks other causes of malnutrition. Further food subsidisation even to the poor is a costly proposition. The alternative and most precise way to target food and nutrition is through monitoring of health posts and schools. Nutrition monitiring in health/family welfare programmes or in schools can identify under-nourished children or their mothers. Through them the hunger families can be identified. This is a better way of identifying the real hungry. These hungry families can be provided with food or purchasing power through food stamps[2] which are though costly are usually cheaper than food subsidy schemes[3]. Food stamps or vouchers can enables the hungry families to obtain free food in ration shops or from other outlets. Food stamps are usually better targeted to needy poor. The food stamp scheme is highly successful in countries like Srilanka and Malaysia. The implementation of this scheme in rural areas for the benefit of poor is likely to slove the problems of nutritional inadequacy which are presently faced by the poor.

Though food entitlement can be provided to the malnourished famlies through targeting in schools or other community based programmes, yet targeting through the health system has additional advantages. The health post can identify whether malnutrition is due to disease, lack of micro-nutrients or food. It can initiate treatment of the disease and remedy nutrient deficiencies with food or other supplements. Primary health services can be empowered to write 'prescriptions' for food for entire families once they have identified the hungry child or mother. Such power can make the primary health care system more attractive to users.[4]

Besides the direct public action or supported programme, the growth based programmes encompassing various catalysts of growth needed in the block can be simultaneously emphasised. The programmes like extension of irrigation facilities, establishment of non-farm occupation and small industries, improvement of infrastructure like road and transport, power etc., improvemnt of health care and education etc., are needed in an underdeveloped block like Begunia. The hungry people can derive benefit both directly and indirectly through such development programmes.

To conclude, the most effective way of eliminating hunger in Begunia block is to provide wage-employment to the poorest of the poor so as to increase their income and employment. Besides, the increase in food entitlement through food stamps to the hungry is essential. Therefore, a policy that combines wage-employment with food supplementation is the best measure for eliminating hunger. Besides the other entitlements that can help in eliminating endemic deprivation and undernutrition include basic health care and elementary education. They also include other necessities such as safe drinking water, living space and basic sanitation. These are direct short-term measures to tackle immediate problems of deprivation. At the same-time, a long-term programme of over-all development of the block should be undertaken in making adequate investment in growth inducing factors like irrigation, improvement of infrastructure, non-farm occupation etc., which have been spelled out in greater detail in specific measures for development. All these will bring about a significant change in the economic land scape of the block, which may help the poor to take up some productive avocations to increase their income and level of living.

NOTES

1. See, V.M. Daṇḍekar, 'Agriculture, Employment and Poverty', *Economic and Political Weekly*, Review of Agriculture, 21,1986.
2. Food Stamps are similar to ration schemes, except that the quota is measured in nominal currency units rather than commodity weight.
3. See, H.P. Binswanger and P. Landell-Mills, 'The World Bank's Strategy for Reducing Poverty and Hunger', *Environmentally Sustainable Development Studies and Monograph Series No. 4.* The World Bank, 1995, pp. 35-36.
4. *Ibid,* p. 37.

Select Biblography

1. Books & Journals

Basu, Kaushik (1995), 'The Elimination of Endemic Poverty in South Asia: Some Policy Options; in J. Dreze, A. Sen and A. Bussain (eds.), *The Political Economy of Hunger,* Oxford University Press, New York.

Bhalla, G.S. (1995). *Economic Liberalisation and Indian Agriculture*, Concept Publishing Company, New Delhi.

Chhabra, Hari Sharan (1996), 'War Against Hunger in Africa', *World Focus,* Vol.17, No.9, Sept.

Dandekar, V.M. (1996), 'Agriculture, Employment and Poverty', *Economic and Political Weekly,* Review of Agriculture, Vol. 21

Dasgupta,Biplab (1995),'Institutional Reforms and Poverty Allevia tion in West Bengal', *EPW, V*ol. 30, Nos. 41 & 42, Oct.14-21.

Dev, S. Mahendra (1995), 'Alleviating Poverty: Maharashtra Employment Guarantee Scheme,' *EPW,* Vol. 30, Nos.41 & 42, Oct.14-21.

(1996),'PDS Vs EGS __ A Tale of Two States', *EPW,* Vol. 31, No.27, July 6.

Dreze, Jean and Sen, Amartya (1989), *Hunger and Public Action,* Oxford University Press, New York.

Gupta, S.K. (1993), *Development of Agro-Industries: Problems and Prospects,* Deep and Deep Publications, New Delhi.

Hashim,S.R .(1996), 'Dimensions of Poverty and Approach to Pov erty Alleviation,' *Yojana*, Vol. 40, No.11 November.

Hirway,India (1995),'Selective Development and Widening Disparities in Gujarat,' *EPW*, Vol.30, Nos. 41 & 42, Oct.14-21.

Kannan, K.P. (1995), 'Declining Incidence of Rural Poverty in Kerala', *EPW*, Vol. 30, 41 & 42, Oct.14-21.

Khullar, P.K.(1996), 'India; World's Food Basket,' *The Economic Times*, Nov. 6.

Madhok,Sujata (1996), 'World Food Summit: Half a Loaf for the Hungry,' *Kurukshetra*, December.

Mathur, Kuldeep (1995), 'Politics and Implementation of Integrated Rural Development Programme', *EPW* , Vol,30, Nos. 41 & 42, Oct.14-21.

Mishra,K.M. (1990), *Irrigation and Economic Development*, Ashish Publishing House, New Delhi.

Misra, Baidyanath (1992), 'Rural Employment, Planning and Development of Orissa, '*Vision*, July-Dec.

__ (1997), *Economic Profile of India*, A.P.H. Publishing Corpo ration, New Delhi.

Misra, Girish (1996), 'Food Security for All', *World Focus*, Vol 17, No. 9 Sept.

Misra, S.N. and Sahu, B.K. (1997), *Multi-Agency System and Rural Development in India*, Spellbound Publications Pvt. Ltd., Rohtak.

Parikh, Kirit S.(1996), 'Reaching the Poor through PDS,' *The Economic Times*, Vol. 36, No. 208 , Calcutta, Sept. 30.

__ (1996), 'Hunger Amidst Abundance,' *The Economic Times* Calcutta, Nov. 25.

__ (1997), 'Do We Really Care for the Poor?' *The Economic Times*, Calcutta, June 23.

Parthasarathy, G. (1995), 'Public Intervention and Rural Poverty: Case Study of Non-Sustainable Reduction in Andhra Pradesh', *EPW,* Vol. 30, Nos.41 & 42, Oct.14-21.

Radhakrishnan, R. (1996), 'Food Trends, PDS and Food Security,' Indian *Journal of Agricultural Economic,* Vol. 51.

Rao, K.Madhava and Subbarao, D. (1997), 'Poverty Ration: Federal Dimensions,' *The Economic Times,* Calcutta, Jan. 28.

Rath , Nilakantha (1996), 'Poverty in India — Revisited,' *Indian Journal of Agricultural Economics,* Vol. 51, Nos.1&2, Jan-June.

Sagar, Vidya (1995), 'Public Intervention for Poverty Alleviation in Harsh Agro-Climatic Environment: Case Study of Rajasthan,' *EPW,* Vol. 30, Nos. 41 & 42. Oct.14-21.

Satapathy, Trilochan (1984), *Irrigation and Economic Development,* Ashish Publishing House, New Delhi.

Sen, Abhijit (1996), 'Economic Reforms, Employment and Poverty. — Trends and Options,' *EPW,* Special Issue, December.

Shankar, Vinay (1996), 'Panchayats and Food Security,' *World Focus*, Vol.17, No, 9 Sept.

Sharma, A.N.(1995), 'Political Economy of Poverty in Bihar', *EPW,* Vol. 30, Nos. 41 & 42, Oct. 14-21.

Sharma, Devinder (1996), 'Rising Food Insecurity,' *World Focus,* Vol. 17, No.9, Sept.

Shiva, Vandana (1996), 'Rising Food Insecurity', *World Focus,* Vol.17, No. 9, Sept.

Shylendra, H.S. (1996), 'Institutional Reform and Rural Poor: A Study on the Distributional Performance of a Regional Rural Bank', *Indian Journal of Agricultural Economics,* Vol. 51, No. 3, July-Sept.

Sitaraman, V and Krishnakumar, T. (1996), 'Minimum Needs of Poor and Priorities Attached to Them, '*EPW,* Special issue, Dec.

Swaminathan, M.S. (1996), 'Sustainable Agriculture and a Hunger-Free India,'*Agricultural Situation in India,* August.

__ (1996), 'Towards a Hunger-Free India', *Kurukshetra Dec.*

Venkaiah, V. (1987), *Impact of Agro-Based Industries on Rural Economy,* Himalaya Publishing House, Bombay.

Vyasula,Vinod (1995), 'Management of Poverty Alleviation Programmes in Karnataka: An Overview,' *EPW,* Vol. 30, Nos. 41 & 42, Oct.

Vyas,V.S. and Bhargava, P.(1995), 'Public Intervention for Poverty Alleviation: An Overview', *EPW,* Vol. 30, Nos. 41 & 42, Oct. 14-21.

II. Reports and Government Publications

Binswanger, H.P. and Landell-Mills, P.(1995), *The World Bank's Strategy for Reducing Poverty and Hunger,* Environmentally Sustainable Development studies and Monographs Series, No.4, The World Bank.

Government of India, *Annual Report:* 1995-96, Ministries of Rural Areas and Employment, New Delhi.

Government of Orissa (1995*), Economic Survey: 1994-95,* Direct orate of Economics and Statistics.

Gupta, S.P. (undated), *Evaluation of I.R.D. and E.R.R.P. Programmes in the District of Sambalpur*. (sponsored by Government of Orissa), P.G. Department of Economics, Sambalpur University, Burla

Mallik, R.M. Padhi, S. and Meher, S. (1994), *Irrigation Systems in Orissa: Its Impact on Agricultural Development*, Interim Report (submitted to ICAR), NRC Centre for Development Studies, Bhubaneswar.

Meher, R.K. (1992), *Problems and Prospects of Handloom Industry in Orissa*, NKC Centre for Development Studies, Bhubaneswar.

Meher, Shibalal (1987), *Income and Employment Generated Through IRDP During the Sixth Five Year Plan: A Comparative Study in Two Blocks of Sambalpur District, M.Phil Dissertation,* Sambalpur University

Operations Research Group (1984), *Socio-Economic Appraisal of Minor Irrigation Projects __ A Pilot Study in Dhenkanal Distict*, Bhubaneswar.

Walters, Harry (1994). 'Overcoming Global Hunger: An Issues Paper' in Nancy Birdshall (ed), *Macro-economic Reform: Its Impact on Poverty and Hunger,* Environmentally Sustainable Development Proceeding series, No.3, The World Bank.

Water and Management Institute (WALMI) (1998), *Report on Socio-Economic Bench Mark Survey in Action Research Area of Kuanria Medium Irrigation Project,* Orissa, Bhubaneswar.

Webb, Patric and Braum, J.V. (1994), 'Ending Hunger Soon: Concepts and Priorities',in Nancy Birdshall (ed).*Macro-economic Reform: Its Impact on Poverty and Hunger*, Envir onmentally Sustainable Development Proceeding, Series No. 3, The World Bank.

World Bank (1990), *World Development Report: 1990,* Oxford University Press, Washington, D.C.

World Bank (1994), *Overcoming Global Hunger,* Washington, D.C.

Index

❑❑❑